THE

POETICAL WORKS

OF

JAMES MONTGOMERY.

VOL. III.

(1)

THE

POETICAL WORKS

OF

JAMES MONTGOMERY.

IN FIVE VOLUMES.

VOL. III.

GREENLAND. MISCELLANEOUS POEMS. NARRATIVES.
TRANSLATIONS FROM DANTE.

BOSTON:
LITTLE, BROWN AND COMPANY.
NEW YORK: PHINNEY, BLAKEMAN AND MASON.
M.DCCC.LX.

CAMBRIDGE:
ALLEN AND FARNHAM, PRINTERS.

CONTENTS

OF

THE THIRD VOLUME.

GREENLAND.

MISCELLANEOUS POEMS.

NARRATIVES.

TRANSLATIONS FROM DANTE.

GREENLAND.

A POEM, IN FIVE CANTOS.

PREFACE.

In the following Poem the Author frankly acknowledges that he has so far failed, as to be under the necessity of sending it forth incomplete, or suppressing it altogether. Why he has not done the latter is of little importance to the public, which will assuredly award him no more credit than his performance, taken as it is, can command; while the consequences of his temerity, or his misfortune, must remain wholly with himself.

The original plan was intended to embrace the most prominent events in the annals of ancient and modern Greenland; — incidental descriptions of whatever is sublime or picturesque in the seasons and scenery, or peculiar in the superstitions, manners, and character of the natives, — with a rapid retrospect of that moral revolution which the Gospel has wrought among these people by reclaiming them, almost universally, from dark idolatry and savage ignorance.

Of that part of the projected poem which is here exhibited, the first three cantos contain a sketch of the history of the ancient Moravian Church, its revival in the early part of the eighteenth century, the origin of the missions by that people to Greenland, and the voyage of the first three brethren who went thither in 1733. The fourth canto refers principally to traditions concerning the Norwegian colonies, which are said to have existed, on both shores of Greenland, from the tenth century to the fifteenth. In the fifth canto the author has attempted, in a series of episodes, to sum up and exemplify the chief causes of the extinction of those colonies, and the abandonment of Greenland for several centuries by European voyagers. Although this canto is entirely a work of imagination, the fiction has not been adopted merely as a substitute for lost facts, but as a vehicle for illustrating some of the most splendid and striking phenomena of the climate, for which a more appropriate place might not have been found, even if the poem had been carried to a successful conclusion.

The principal subjects introduced in the course of the poem will be found in Crantz's histories of the Brethren and of Greenland, or in Risler's Narratives, extracted from the records of the ancient *Unitas Fratrum*, or United Brethren. To the accounts of Iceland, by various travellers, the author is also much indebted.

Sheffield, *March* 27, 1819.

GREENLAND.

CANTO FIRST.

The first three Moravian Missionaries are represented as on their Voyage to Greenland, in the Year 1733. — Sketch of the Descent, Establishment, Persecutions, Extinction, and Revival of the Church of the United Brethren from the tenth to the beginning of the eighteenth Century. — The Origin of their Missions to the West Indies and to Greenland.

THE moon is watching in the sky; the stars
Are swiftly wheeling on their golden cars;
Ocean, outstretch't with infinite expanse,
Serenely slumbers in a glorious trance;
The tide o'er which no troubling spirits breathe,
Reflects a cloudless firmament beneath;
Where, poised as in the centre of a sphere,
A ship above and ship below appear;
A double image, pictured on the deep,
The vessel o'er its shadow seems to sleep;
Yet, like the host of heaven, that never rest,
With evanescent motion to the west,
The pageant glides through loneliness and night,
And leaves behind a rippling wake of light.

Hark! through the calm and silence of the scene,
Slow, solemn, sweet, with many a pause between,
Celestial music swells along the air!
— No! — 't is the evening hymn of praise and prayer
From yonder deck; where, on the stern retired,
Three humble voyagers, with looks inspired,
And hearts, enkindled with a holier flame,
Than ever lit to empire or to fame,
Devoutly stand: — their choral accents rise
On wings of harmony beyond the skies;
And 'midst the songs, that Seraph-Minstrels sing,
Day without night, to their immortal King,
These simple strains, — which erst Bohemian hills
Echo'd to pathless woods and desert rills;
Now heard from Shetland's azure bound, — are known
In heaven; and He, who sits upon the throne
In human form, with mediatorial power,
Remembers Calvary, and hails the hour,
When, by the' Almighty Father's high decree,
The utmost north to Him shall bow the knee,
And, won by love, an untamed rebel-race
Kiss the victorious Sceptre of His grace.
Then to *His* eye, whose instant glance pervades
Heaven's heights, Earth's circle, Hell's profoundest shades,
Is there a group more lovely than those three
Night-watching Pilgrims on the lonely sea?
Or to *His* ear, that gathers in one sound
The voices of adoring worlds around,

Comes there a breath of more delightful praise
Than the faint notes his poor disciples raise,
Ere on the treacherous main they sink to rest,
Secure as leaning on their Master's breast?

They sleep: but memory wakes; and dreams array
Night in a lively masquerade of day;
The land they seek, the land they leave behind,
Meet on mid-ocean in the plastic mind:
One brings forsaken home and friends so nigh,
That tears in slumber swell the' unconscious eye;
The other opens, with prophetic view,
Perils, which e'en their fathers never knew,
(Though school'd by suffering, long inured to toil,
Outcasts and exiles from their natal soil;)
— Strange scenes, strange men; untold, untried distress;
Pain, hardships, famine, cold, and nakedness,
Diseases; death in every hideous form,
On shore, at sea, by fire, by flood, by storm;
Wild beasts and wilder men; — unmoved with fear,
Health, comfort, safety, life, they count not dear,
May they but hope a Saviour's love to show,
And warn one spirit from eternal woe;
Nor will they faint; nor can they strive in vain,
Since thus — to live is Christ, to die is gain.

'T is morn: — the bathing moon her lustre shrouds;
Wide o'er the East impends an arch of clouds,
That spans the ocean; — while the infant dawn
Peeps through the portal o'er the liquid lawn,

That ruffled by an April gale appears,
Between the gloom and splendor of the spheres,
Dark-purple as the moorland-heath, when rain
Hangs in low vapors o'er the autumnal plain:
Till the full Sun, resurgent from the flood,
Looks on the waves and turns them into blood;
But quickly kindling, as his beams aspire,
The lambent billows play in forms of fire.
— Where is the Vessel? — Shining through the light,
Like the white sea-fowl's horizontal flight,
Yonder she wings, and skims, and cleaves her way
Through refluent foam and iridescent spray.

Lo! on the deck, with patriarchal grace,
Heaven in his bosom opening o'er his face,
Stands Christian David; — venerable name!
Bright in the records of celestial fame,
On earth obscure; — like some sequester'd star,
That rolls in its Creator's beams afar,
Unseen by man; till telescopic eye,
Sounding the blue abysses of the sky,
Draws forth its hidden beauty into light,
And adds a jewel to the crown of night.
Though hoary with the multitude of years,
Unshorn of strength, between his young compeers,
He towers; — with faith, whose boundless glance can see
Time's shadows brightening through eternity;
Love, — God's own love in his pure breast enshrined;
Love, — love to man the magnet of his mind;

Sublimer schemes maturing in his thought
Than ever statesman plann'd or warrior wrought;
While, with rejoicing tears, and rapturous sighs,
To heaven ascends their morning sacrifice.*

Whence are the pilgrims? whither would they roam?
Greenland their port; — Moravia *was* their home.
Sprung from a race of martyrs; men who bore
The cross on many a Golgotha, of yore;
When first Sclavonian tribes the truth received,
And princes at the price of thrones believed; †
— When WALDO, flying from the' apostate west, ‡
In German wilds his righteous cause confess'd;
— When WICKLIFFE, like a rescuing Angel, found
The dungeon where the word of God lay bound,

* The names of the first three Moravian missionaries to Greenland were Christian David, Matthew Stach, and Christian Stach.

† The Church of the United Brethren (first established under that name about the year 1460) traces its descent from the Sclavonian branch of the Greek Church, which was spread throughout Bohemia and Moravia, as well as the ancient Dalmatia. The Bulgarians were once the most powerful tribe of the Sclavic nations; and among them the Gospel was introduced in the ninth century. — See additional note (A) in the Appendix.

‡ With the Waldenses, the Bohemian and Moravian Churches, which never properly submitted to the authority of the Pope, held intimate communion for ages; and from Stephen, the last bishop of the Waldenses, in 1467, the United Brethren received their episcopacy. Almost immediately afterwards, those ancient confessors of the truth were dispersed by a cruel persecution, and Stephen himself suffered martyrdom, being burnt as a heretic at Vienna.

Unloosed its chains, and led it by the hand,
In its own sunshine, through his native land: *
— When HUSS, the victim of perfidious foes,
To heaven upon a fiery chariot rose;
And ere he vanish'd, with a prophet's breath,
Foretold the' immortal triumphs of his death: †
— When ZISKA, burning with fanatic zeal,
Exchanged the Spirit's sword for patriot steel,
And through the heart of Austria's thick array
To Tabor's summit stabb'd resistless way;
But there (as if transfigured on the spot
The world's Redeemer stood) his rage forgot;
Deposed his arms and trophies in the dust,
Wept like a babe, and placed in God his trust,
While prostrate warriors kiss'd the hallow'd ground,
And lay, like slain, in silent ranks around: ‡

* Wickliffe's writings were early translated into the Bohemian tongue, and eagerly read by the devout and persecuted people, who never had given up the Bible in their own language, nor consented to perform their church service in Latin. Archbishop Sbinek, of Prague, ordered the works of Wickliffe to be burnt by the hands of the hangman. He himself could scarcely read!

† It is well known that John Huss (who might be called a disciple of our Wickliffe), though furnished with a safe-conduct by the Emperor Sigismund, was burnt by a decree of the council of Constance. Several sayings predictive of retribution to the priests, and reformation in the Church, are recorded, as being uttered by him in his last hours. Among others: — "A hundred years hence," said he, addressing his judges, "ye shall render an account of your doings to God and to me." Luther appeared at the period thus indicated.

‡ After the martyrdom of John Huss, his followers and coun-

— When mild GREGORIUS, in a lowlier field,
As brave a witness, as unwont to yield
As ZISKA's self, with patient footsteps trod
A path of suffering, like the Son of God,
And nobler palms, by meek endurance won,
Than if his sword had blazed from sun to sun: *
Though nature fail'd him on the racking wheel,
He felt the joys which parted spirits feel;
Rapt into bliss from ecstasy of pain,
Imagination wander'd o'er a plain:
Fair in the midst, beneath a morning sky,
A tree its ample branches bore on high,
With fragrant bloom, and fruit delicious hung,
While birds beneath the foliage fed and sung;
All glittering to the sun with diamond dew,
O'er sheep and kine a breezy shade it threw;
A lovely boy, the child of hope and prayer,
With crook and shepherd's pipe, was watching there
At hand three venerable forms were seen,
In simple garb, with apostolic mien,
Who mark'd the distant fields convulsed with strife,
— The guardian Cherubs of that Tree of Life;

trymen took up arms for the maintenance of their civil and religious liberties. The first and most distinguished of theii leaders was John Ziska. He seized possession of a high mountain, which he fortified, and called Tabor. Here he and his people (who were hence called Taborites) worshipped God ac cording to their consciences and his holy word; while in the plains they fought and conquered their persecutors and enemies.

* See note (B) in the Appendix, for a brief account of this Gregory, and an illustration of the lines that follow concerning his trance and vision while he lay upon the rack.

Not armed like Eden's host, with flaming brands,
Alike to friends and foes they stretch their hands,
In sign of peace, and while Destruction spread
His path with carnage, welcomed all who fled:
— When poor COMENIUS, with his little flock,
Escaped the wolves, and from the boundary rock,
Cast o'er Moravian hills a look of woe,
Saw the green vales expand, the waters flow,
And happier years revolving in his mind,
Caught every sound that murmur'd on the wind;
As if his eye could never thence depart,
As if his ear were seated in his heart,
And his full soul would thence a passage break,
To leave the body, for his country's sake;
While on his knees he pour'd the fervent prayer,
That God would make that martyr-land his care,
And nourish in its ravaged soil a root
Of GREGOR'S Tree, to bear perennial fruit.*

His prayer was heard: — that Church, through ages past,
Assail'd and rent by persecution's blast;

* John Amos Comenius, one of the most learned as well as pious men of his age, was minister of the Brethren's congregation at Fulneck, in Moravia, from 1618 to 1627, when the Protestant nobility and clergy being expatriated, he fled with a part of his people through Silesia into Poland. On the summit of the mountains forming the boundary, he turned his sorrowful eyes towards Bohemia and Moravia, and kneeling down with his brethren there, implored God, with many tears, that he would not take away the light of his holy word from those two provinces, but preserve in them a remnant for himself. A remnant *was* saved. — See Appendix, note (C).

Whose sons no yoke could crush, no burden tire,
Unawed by dungeons, tortures, sword, and fire,
(Less proof against the world's alluring wiles,
Whose frowns have weaker terrors than its smiles ;)
— That Church o'erthrown, dispersed, unpeopled, dead,
Oft from the dust of ruin raised her head,
And rallying round her feet, as from their graves,
Her exiled orphans, hid in forest-caves ;
Where, 'midst the fastnesses of rocks and glens,
Banded like robbers, stealing from their dens,
By night they met, their holiest vows to pay,
As if their deeds were dark, and shunn'd the day ;
While Christ's revilers, in his seamless robe,
And parted garments, flaunted round the globe ;
From east to west while priestcraft's banners flew,
And harness'd kings his iron chariot drew ;
— That Church advanced triumphant, o'er the ground,
Where all her conquering martyrs had been crown'd,
Fearless her foe's whole malice to defy,
And worship God in liberty, — or die :
For truth and conscience oft she pour'd her blood,
And firmest in the fiercest conflicts stood,
Wresting from bigotry the proud control
Claim'd o'er the sacred empire of the soul,
Where God, the judge of all, should fill the throne,
And reign, as in his universe, alone.*

* See note (D) in the Appendix.

'Twas thus through centuries she rose and fell;
At length victorious seem'd the gates of hell;
But founded on a rock, which cannot move —
The' eternal rock of her Redeemer's love —
That Church, which Satan's legions thought destroy'd,
Her name extinct, her place for ever void,
Alive once more, respired her native air,
But found no freedom for the voice of prayer:
Again the cowl'd oppressor clank'd his chains,
Flourish'd his scourge, and threaten'd bonds and pains,
(His arm enfeebled could no longer kill,
But in his heart he was a murderer still:)
Then CHRISTIAN DAVID, strengthen'd from above,
Wise as the serpent, harmless as the dove;
Bold as a lion on his Master's part,
In zeal a seraph, and a child in heart:
Pluck'd from the gripe of antiquated laws,
— Even as a mother from the felon jaws
Of a lean wolf, that bears her babe away,
With courage beyond nature, rends the prey,
— The little remnant of that ancient race:
Far in Lusatian woods they found a place;
There — where the sparrow builds her busy nest,
And the clime-changing swallow loves to rest,
Thine altar, God of Hosts! — *there* still appear
The tribes to worship, unassail'd by fear;
Not like their fathers, vex'd from age to age
By blatant Bigotry's insensate rage,

Abroad in every place, — in every hour
Awake, alert, and ramping to devour.
No; peaceful as the spot where Jacob slept,
And guard all night the journeying angels kept,
Herrnhut yet stands amidst her shelter'd bowers;
— The Lord hath set his watch upon her towers.*

Soon, homes of humble form, and structure rude,
Raised sweet society in solitude:
And the lorn traveller there, at fall of night,
Could trace from distant hills the spangled light,
Which now from many a cottage window stream'd,
Or in full glory round the chapel beam'd;
While hymning voices, in the silent shade,
Music of all his soul's affections made;
Where through the trackless wilderness erewhile,
No hospitable ray was known to smile;
Or if a sudden splendor kindled joy,
'T was but a meteor dazzling to destroy:

* In 1721 (ninety-four years after the flight of Comenius), the Church of the United Brethren was revived by the persecuted refugees from Moravia (descendants of the old confessors of that name), who were led from time to time by Christian David (himself a Moravian, but educated in the Lutheran persuasion), to settle on an uncultivated piece of land, on an estate belonging to Count Zinzendorf, in Lusatia. Christian David, who was a carpenter, began the work of building a church in this wilderness, by striking his axe into a tree, and exclaiming, — "Here hath the sparrow found an house, and the swallow a nest for herself; even thine altars, O Lord God of Hosts!" They named the settlement Herrnhut, or The Lord's Watch. — See Appendix, note (E).

While the wood echoed to the hollow owl,
The fox's cry, or wolf's lugubrious howl.

Unwearied as the camel, day by day,
Tracks through unwater'd wilds his doleful way,
Yet in his breast a cherish'd draught retains,
To cool the fervid current in his veins,
While from the sun's meridian realms he brings
The gold and gems of Ethiopian kings:
So CHRISTIAN DAVID, spending yet unspent,
On many a pilgrimage of mercy went;
Through all their haunts his suffering brethren sought,
And safely to that land of promise brought;
While in his bosom, on the toilsome road,
A secret well of consolation flow'd,
Fed from the fountain near the eternal throne,
— Bliss to the world unyielded and unknown.

In stillness thus the little Zion rose;
But scarcely found those fugitives repose,
Ere to the West with pitying eyes they turn'd;
Their love to Christ beyond the' Atlantic burn'd.
Forth sped their messengers, content to be
Captives themselves, to cheer captivity;
Soothe the poor Negro with fraternal smiles,
And preach deliverance in those prison-isles,
Where man's most hateful forms of being meet,
— The tyrant and the slave that licks his feet.*

* In 1732, when the congregation at Herrnhut consisted of

O'er Greenland next two youths in secret wept:
And where the sabbath of the dead was kept,
With pious forethought, while their hands prepare
Beds which the living and unborn shall share,
(For man so surely to the dust is brought,
His grave before his cradle may be wrought,)
They told their purpose, each o'erjoy'd to find
His own idea in his brother's mind.
For counsel in simplicity they pray'd,
And vows of ardent consecration made:
— Vows heard in heaven; from that accepted hour,
Their souls were clothed with confidence and power,*
Nor hope deferr'd could quell their hearts' desire;
The bush once kindled grew amidst the fire;

about six hundred persons, including children, the first two missionaries sailed for the Danish island of St. Thomas, to preach the Gospel to the negroes; and such was their devotion to the good work, that being told that they could not have intercourse otherwise with the objects of their Christian compassion, they determined to sell themselves for slaves on their arrival, and work with the blacks in the plantations. But this sacrifice was not required. Many thousand negroes have since been truly converted in the West Indies.

* Matthew Stach and Frederick Boenisch, two young men being at work together, preparing a piece of ground for a burial-place at Herrnhut, disclosed to each other their distinct desires to offer themselves to the congregation as missionaries to Greenland. They therefore became joint candidates. Considerable delay, however, occurred; and when it was at length determined to attempt the preaching of the Gospel there, Frederick Boenisch being on a distant journey, Christian David was appointed to conduct thither Matthew Stach and his cousin, Christian Stach, who sailed from Copenhagen on the 10th of April, 1733, and landed in Ball's river on the 20th of May following.

But ere its shoots a tree of life became,
Congenial spirits caught the' electric flame;
And for that holy service, young and old,
Their plighted faith and willing names enroll'd;
Eager to change the rest, so lately found,
For life-long labors on barbarian ground;
To break, through barriers of eternal ice,
A vista to the gates of Paradise;
And light beneath the shadow of the pole
The tenfold darkness of the human soul;
To man, — a task more hopeless than to bless
With Indian fruits that arctic wilderness;
With God, — as possible when unbegun
As though the destined miracle were done.

Three chosen candidates at length went forth,
Heralds of mercy to the frozen north;
Like mariners with seal'd instructions sent,
They went in faith, (as childless Abram went
To dwell by sufferance in a land, decreed
The future birthright of his promised seed,)
Unknowing whither; — uninquiring why
Their lot was cast beneath so strange a sky,
Where cloud nor star appear'd, to mortal sense
Pointing the hidden path of Providence,
And all around was darkness to be felt;
— Yet in that darkness light eternal dwelt:
They knew, — and 't was enough for them to know,
The still small voice that whisper'd them to go;
For He, who spake by that mysterious voice,
Inspired their will, and made His call their choice,

See the swift vessel bounding o'er the tide,
That wafts with Christian David for their guide,
Two young Apostles on their joyful way
To regions in the twilight verge of day:
Freely they quit the clime that gave them birth,
Home, kindred, friendship, all they loved on earth;
What things were gain before, accounting loss,
And glorying in the shame, they bear the cross;
—Not as the Spaniard, on his flag unfurl'd,
A bloody omen through a Pagan world:
—Not the vain image, which the Devotee
Clasps as the God of his idolatry;
But in their hearts, to Greenland's western shore,
That dear memorial of their Lord they bore;
Amidst the wilderness to lift the sign
Of wrath appeased by sacrifice divine;
And bid a serpent-stung and dying race
Look on their Healer, and be saved by grace.

END OF CANTO I.

CANTO SECOND.

Hopes and Fears. — The Brethren pursue their Voyage. — A Digression on Iceland

WHAT are thine hopes, Humanity! — thy fears?
Poor voyager, upon this flood of years,
Whose tide, unturning, hurries to the sea
Of dark unsearchable eternity,
The fragile skiffs, in which thy children sail
A day, an hour, a moment, with the gale,
Then vanish; — gone like eagles on the wind,
Or fish in waves, that yield and close behind?
Thine Hopes, — lost anchors buried in the deep,
That rust, through storm and calm, in iron sleep;
Whose cables, loose aloft and fix'd below,
Rot with the sea-weed, floating to and fro!
Thy Fears — are wrecks that strew the fatal surge,
Whose whirlpools swallow, or whose currents urge
Adventurous barks on rocks, that lurk at rest,
Where the blue halcyon builds her foam-light nest;
Or strand them on illumined shoals, that gleam
Like drifted gold in summer's cloudless beam:
Thus would thy race, beneath their parent's eye,
Live without knowledge, without prospect die.

But when religion bids her spirit breathe,
And opens bliss above and woe beneath;

When God reveals his march through Nature's night,
His steps are beauty, and his presence light,
His voice is life:—the dead in conscience start;
They feel a new creation in the heart.
Ah! then, Humanity, thy hopes, thy fears,
How changed, how wondrous!—On this tide of years,
Though the frail barks, in which thine offspring sail
Their day, their hour, their moment with the gale,
Must perish;—Shipwreck only sets them free;
With joys unmeasured as eternity,
They ply on seas of glass with golden oars,
And pluck immortal fruits along the shores;
Nor shall *their* cables fail, *their* anchors rust,
Who wait the resurrection of the just:
Moor'd on the Rock of Ages, though decay
Moulder the weak terrestrial frame away,
The trumpet sounds,—and lo! wherever spread,
Earth, air, and ocean render back their dead;
And souls with bodies, spiritual and divine,
In the new heavens, like stars, for ever shine.
These are thine Hopes:—thy Fears what tongue can tell?
Behold them graven on the gates of Hell:
"The wrath of God abideth here: his breath
Kindled the flames:—*this* is the second death."
'Twas Mercy wrote the lines of judgment there;
None who from earth can read them may despair!
Man!—let the warning strike presumption dumb;—
Awake, arise, escape the wrath to come;
No resurrection from *that* grave shall be;
The worm within is—immortality.

The terrors of Jehovah, and his grace,
The Brethren bear to earth's remotest race.
And now, exulting on their swift career,
The northern waters narrowing in the rear,
They rise upon the' Atlantic flood, that rolls
Shoreless and fathomless between the poles,
Whose waves the east and western world divide,
Then gird the globe with one circumfluent tide;
For mighty Ocean, by whatever name
Known to vain man, is everywhere the same,
And deems all regions by his gulfs enbraced
But vassal tenures of his sovereign waste.
Clear shines the sun; the surge, intensely blue,
Assumes by day heaven's own aerial hue:
Buoyant and beautiful, as through a sky,
On balanced wings, behold the vessel fly;
Invisibly impell'd, as though it felt
A soul, within its heart of oak that dwelt,
Which broke the billows with spontaneous force,
Ruled the free elements, and chose its course.
Not so: — and yet along the trackless realm,
A hand unseen directs the' unconscious helm;
The Power that sojourn'd in the cloud by day,
And fire by night, on Israel's desert way;
That Power the obedient vessel owns: — His will,
Tempest and calm, and death and life, fulfil.

Day following day the current smoothly flows;
Labor is but refreshment from repose;
Perils are vanish'd; every fear resign'd;
Peace walks the waves, Hope carols on the wind;

And Time so sweetly travels o'er the deep,
They feel his motion like the fall of sleep
On weary limbs, that, stretch'd in stillness, seem
To float upon the eddy of a stream,
Then sink, — to wake in some transporting dream.
Thus, while the Brethren far in exile roam,
Visions of Greenland show their future home.
— Now a dark speck, but brightening as it flies,
A vagrant sea-fowl glads their eager eyes;
How lovely, from the narrow deck to see
The meanest link of nature's family,
Which makes us feel, in dreariest solitude,
Affinity with all that breathe renew'd:
At once a thousand kind emotions start,
And the blood warms and mantles round the heart!
— O'er the ship's lee, the waves in shadow seen,
Change from deep indigo to beryl green,
And wreaths of frequent weed, that slowly float,
Land to the watchful mariner denote:
Ere long the pulse beats quicker through his breast,
When, like a range of evening clouds at rest,
Iceland's grey cliffs and ragged coast he sees,
But shuns them, leaning on the southern breeze;
And while they vanish far in distance, tells
Of lakes of fire and necromancers' spells.

Strange Isle! a moment to poetic gaze
Rise in thy majesty of rocks and bays,
Glens, fountains, caves, that seem not things of earth,
But the wild shapes of some prodigious birth;

As if the kraken, monarch of the sea,
Wallowing abroad in his immensity,
By polar storms and lightning shafts assail'd, [fail'd;
Wedged with ice-mountains, here had fought and
Perish'd — and in the petrifying blast,
His hulk became an island rooted fast;*
— Rather, from ocean's dark foundation hurl'd,
Thou art a type of his mysterious world,
Buoy'd on the desolate abyss, to show
What wonders of creation hide below.

Here Hecla's triple peaks, with meteor lights,
Nature's own beacons, cheer hybernal nights:
But when the orient flames in red array,
Like ghosts the spectral splendors flee the day;
Morn at her feet beholds supinely spread
The carcass of the old chimera dead,

* The most horrible of fabulous sea-monsters is the *kraken* or *hafgufa*, which many of the Norway fishers pretend to have seen in part, but none entire. They say, that when they find a place which is at one time eighty or one hundred fathoms deep and at another only twenty or thirty, and also observe a multitude of fishes, allured by a delicious exhalation which the kraken emits, they conclude that there is one below them. They therefore hasten to secure a large draught of the fry around them; but as soon as they perceive the soundings to grow shallower, they scud away, and from a safe distance behold him rising in a chain of ridges and spires, that thicken as they emerge, till they resemble the masts of innumerable vessels moored on a rocky coast. He then riots upon the fish that have been stranded and entangled in the forest of spikes upon his back, and having satiated his hunger, plunges into the depths with a violent agitation of the waters. — See *Crantz's Greenland.*

That wont to vomit flames and molten ore,
Now cleft asunder to the inmost core;
In smouldering heaps, wide wrecks and cinders strown,
Lie like the walls of Sodom overthrown,
(Ere from the face of blushing Nature swept,
And where the city stood the Dead Sea slept;)
While inaccessible, tradition feigns,
To human foot the guarded top remains,
Where birds of hideous shape and doleful note,
Fate's ministers, in livid vapors float.*

Far off, amidst the placid sunshine, glow
Mountains with hearts of fire and crests of snow,
Whose blacken'd slopes with deep ravines entrench'd,
Their thunders silenced, and their lightnings quench'd,
Still the slow heat of spent eruptions breathe,
While embryo earthquakes swell their wombs beneath.

Hark! from yon caldron cave, the battle sound
Of fire and water warring under ground;
Rack'd on the wheels of an ebullient tide,
Here might some spirit, fallen from bliss, abide,
Such fitful wailings of intense despair,
Such emanating splendors fill the air.†

* Hecla is now the ruins of a volcano. The three peaks are said to be haunted by evil spirits in the shape of birds. The island abounds with volcanic mountains.

† The Geysers, or boiling fountains, of Iceland, have been so frequently and so happily described, that their phenomena are sufficiently familiar to general readers not to require any partic-

— He comes, he comes; thc' infuriate Geyser springs
Up to the firmament on vapory wings;
With breathless awe the mountain glory view;
White whirling clouds his steep ascent pursue.
But lo! a glimpse; — refulgent to the gale,
He starts all naked through his riven veil;
A fountain-column, terrible and bright,
A living, breathing, moving form of light:
From central earth to heaven's meridian thrown,
The mighty apparition towers alone,
Rising, as though for ever he could rise,
Storm and resume his palace in the skies.
All foam, and turbulence, and wrath below;
Around him beams the reconciling bow;
(Signal of peace, whose radiant girdle binds,
Till nature's doom, the waters and the winds;)
While mist and spray, condensed to sudden dews,
The air illumine with celestial hues,
As if the bounteous sun were raining down
The richest gems of his imperial crown.
In vain the spirit wrestles to break free,
Foot-bound to fathomless captivity;
A power unseen, by sympathetic spell
For ever working, — to his flinty cell,

ular illustration here. The Great Geyser, according to Dr. Henderson (the latest traveller who has published an account of Iceland), is seventy-eight feet in perpendicular depth, and from eight to ten feet in diameter: the mouth is a considerable basin, from which the column of boiling water is ejaculated to various heights; sometimes exceeding one hundred feet.

Recalls him from the ramparts of the spheres;
He yields, collapses, lessens, disappears;
Darkness receives him in her vague abyss,
Around whose verge light froth and bubbles hiss,
While the low murmurs of the refluent tide
Far into subterranean silence glide,
The eye still gazing down the dread profound,
When the bent ear hath wholly lost the sound.
— But is he slain and sepulchred? — Again
The deathless giant sallies from his den,
Scales with recruited strength the ethereal walls,
Struggles afresh for liberty — and falls.
Yes, and for liberty the fight renew'd,
By day, by night, undaunted, unsubdued,
He shall maintain, till Iceland's solid base
Fail, and the mountains vanish from its face.

And can these fail? — Of Alpine height and
mould
Schapta's unshaken battlements behold;
His throne an hundred hills; his sun-crown'd head
Resting on clouds; his robe of shadow spread
O'er half the isle; he pours from either hand
An unexhausted river through the land, [green,
On whose fair banks, through valleys warm and
Cattle and flocks, and homes, and spires are seen.
Here Nature's earthquake pangs were never felt;
Here in repose hath man for ages dwelt;
The everlasting mountain seems to say,
"I am, — and I shall never pass away."

Yet fifty winters, and with huge uproar,
Thy pride shall perish ; — thou shalt be no more ;
Amidst chaotic ruins on the plain,
Those cliffs, these waters shall be sought in vain ! *
— Through the dim vista of unfolding years,
A pageant of portentous woe appears.
Yon rosy groups, with golden locks, at play,
I see them, — few, decrepit, silent, grey ;
Their fathers all at rest beneath the sod,
Whose flowerless verdure marks the House of God,
Home of the living and the dead ; — where meet
Kindred and strangers, in communion sweet,
When dawns the Sabbath on the block-built pile ;
The kiss of peace, the welcome, and the smile
Go round ; till comes the Priest, a father there,
And the bell knolls his family to prayer ;
Angels might stoop from thrones in heaven, to be
Co-worshippers in such a family,
Whom from their nooks and dells, where'er they roam,
The Sabbath gathers to their common home.
Oh ! I would stand a keeper at this gate
Rather than reign with kings in guilty state ;

* This imaginary prophecy (1733) was fulfilled just fifty years afterwards, in 1783. The *Schapta*, *Schaptka*, or *Shaftar Yokul* and its adjacencies were the subjects of the most tremendous volcanic devastation on record. Two rivers were sunk or evaporated, and their channels filled up with lava; many villages were utterly destroyed; and one fourth part of the island rendered nearly uninhabitable. Famine and pestilence followed.

A day in such serene enjoyment spent
Were worth an age of splendid discontent!
— But whither am I hurried from my theme?
Schapta returns on the prophetic dream.

From eve till morn strange meteors streak the pole;
At cloudless noon mysterious thunders roll,
As if below both shore and ocean hurl'd
From deep convulsions of the nether world;
Anon the river, boiling from its bed,
Shall leap its bounds and o'er the lowlands spread,
Then waste in exhalation, — leaving void
As its own channel, utterly destroy'd,
Fields, gardens, dwellings, churches, and their graves,
All wreck'd or disappearing with the waves.
The fugitives that 'scape this instant death
Inhale slow pestilence with every breath;
Mephitic streams from Schapta's mouldering breast
With livid horror shall the air infest;
And day shall glare so foully on the sight,
Darkness were refuge from the curse of light.
Lo! far among the glaciers, wrapt in gloom,
The red precursors of approaching doom,
Scatter'd and solitary founts of fire,
Unlock'd by hands invisible, aspire;
Ere long more rapidly than eye can count,
Above, beneath, they multiply, they mount,
Converge, condense, — a crimson phalanx form,
And range aloft in one unbounded storm;

From heaven's red roof the fierce reflections throw
A sea of fluctuating light below.
— Now the whole army of destroyers, fleet
As whirlwinds, terrible as lightnings, meet;
The mountains melt like wax along their course,
When downward, pouring with resistless force,
Through the void channel where the river roll'd,
To ocean's verge their flaming march they hold;
While blocks of ice, and crags of granite rent,
Half-fluid ore, and rugged minerals blent,
Float on the gulf, till molten or immersed,
Or in explosive thunderbolts dispersed.
Thus shall the Schapta, towering on the brink
Of unknown jeopardy, in ruin sink;
And this wild paroxysm of frenzy past,
At her own work shall Nature stand aghast.

Look on this desolation: — mark yon brow,
Once adamant, a cone of ashes now:
Here rivers swampt; there valleys levell'd, plains
O'erwhelm'd; — one black-red wilderness remains,
One crust of lava, through whose cinder-heat
The pulse of buried streams is felt to beat;
These from the frequent fissures, eddying white,
Sublimed to vapor, issued forth like light
Amidst the sulphury fumes, that drear and dun,
Poison the atmosphere and blind the sun.
Above, as if the sky had felt the stroke
Of that volcano, and consumed to smoke,

One cloud appears in heaven, and one alone,
Hung round the dark horizon's craggy zone,
Forming at once the vast encircling wall,
And the dense roof of some Tartarean hall,
Propt by a thousand pillars, huge and strange,
Fantastic forms that every moment change,
As hissing, surging from the floor beneath,
Volumes of steam the' imprison'd waters breathe.
Then should the sun, ere evening gloom ascend,
Quick from the west the murky curtain rend,
And pour the beauty of his beams, between
These hideous arches, and light up the scene;
At the sweet touch of his transforming rays
With amber lustre all the columns blaze,
And the thick folds of cumbrous fog aloof
Change to rich drapery of celestial woof:
With such enchantment air and earth were fraught,
Beyond the coloring of the wealthiest thought
That Iceland Scalds, transported at the view,
Might deem the legends of their fathers true,
And here behold, illumining the waste,
The palace of immortal Odin placed;
Till rapt imagination joy'd to hear
The neigh of steeds, the clank of armor near,
And saw, in barbarous state, the tables spread
With shadowy food, and compass'd with the dead,
Weary from conflicts, — still the fierce delight
Of spectre-warriors, in the daily fight:
Then while they quaff'd the mead from skulls of foes,
By whirlwind gusts the din of battle rose;

The strife of tongues, the tournament of words
Following the shock of shields, the clash of swords;
Till, gorged and drunken at the' enormous feast,
Awhile their revels and their clamors ceased;
Ceased to the eye and ear; — yet where they lay,
Like sleeping lions, surfeited with prey,
In tawny groups, recumbent through the den,
In dreams the heroes drank and fought again.

Away with such Divinities! their birth
Man's brain-sick superstition, and their mirth
Lust, rapine, cruelty; — their fell employ
God's works and their own votaries to destroy.
— The Runic Bard to nobler themes shall string
His ancient harp, and mightier triumphs sing:
For glorious days are risen on Iceland: — clear
The gospel-trumpet sounds to every ear,
And deep in many a heart the Spirit's voice
Bids the believing soul in hope rejoice.
O'er the stern face of this tempestuous isle,
Though briefly Spring, and Autumn never, smile,
Truth walks with naked foot the' unyielding snows,
And the glad desert blossoms like the rose.
Though earthquakes heave, though torrents drown his cot,
Volcanoes waste his fields, — the peasant's lot
Is blest beyond the destiny of kings:
— Lifting his eyes above sublunar things,
Like dying Stephen, when he saw in prayer
Heaven open'd, and his Saviour beckoning there,

He cries, and clasps his Bible to his breast,
" Let the earth perish, — *here* is not my rest." *

* One of the finest specimens of Icelandic poetry extant is said to be the " Ode to the British and Foreign Bible Society," composed by the Rev. John Thorlakson, of Bœgisà, the translator of Milton's "Paradise Lost" into his native tongue. Of this Ode there is a Latin translation by the learned Iceland Professor, Finn Magnusson. A spirited English version has also appeared. Thorlakson is a venerable old man, and holds church preferment to the amount of six pounds five shillings per annum, out of which he allows a stipend to a curate.

END OF CANTO II.

CANTO THIRD.

The Voyage to Greenland concluded. — A Fog at Sea. — Ice-fields. — Eclipse of the Sun. — The Greenland Fable of Malina and Aninga. — A Storm. — The Ice-blink. — Northern Lights. — The Brethren land.

How speed the faithful witnesses, who bore
The Bible and its hopes to Greenland's shore?
— Like Noah's ark, alone upon the wave
(Of one lost world the' immeasurable grave),
Yonder the ship, a solitary speck,
Comes bounding from the horizon; while on deck
Again imagination rests her wing,
And smoothes her pinions, while the Pilgrims sing
Their vesper oraisons. — The Sun retires,
Not as he wont, with clear and golden fires;
Bewilder'd in a labyrinth of haze,
His orb redoubled, with discolor'd rays,
Struggles and vanishes; — along the deep,
With slow array, expanding vapors creep,
Whose folds, in twilight's yellow glare uncurl'd,
Present the dreams of an unreal world;
Islands in air suspended; marching ghosts
Of armies, shapes of castles, winding coasts,
Navies at anchor, mountains, woods, and streams,
Where all is strange, and nothing what it seems;
Till deep involving gloom, without a spark
Of star, moon, meteor, desolately dark,

Seals up the vision: — then, the Pilot's fears
Slacken his arm; a doubtful course he steers,
Till morning comes, but comes not clad in light;
Uprisen day is but a paler night,
Revealing not a glimpse of sea or sky;
The ship's circumference bounds the sailor's eye.
So cold and dense the' impervious fog extends,
He might have touch'd the point where being ends;
His bark is all the universe; so void
The scene, — as though creation were destroy'd,
And he and his few mates, of all their race,
Were here becalm'd in everlasting space.*

Silent and motionless, above, below,
The sails all struck, the waves unheard to flow,
In this drear blank of utter solitude,
Where life stands still, no faithless fears intrude;
Through that impervious veil the Brethren see
The face of omnipresent Deity:
Nor Him alone; — whate'er his hand hath made;
His glory in the firmament display'd;
The sun majestic in his course, and sole;
The moon and stars rejoicing round the pole;
Earth o'er its peopled realms and wastes unknown,
Clad in the wealth of every varying zone;
Ocean through all the' enchantment of his forms,
From breathing calms to devastating storms;

* The incidents described in this canto are founded upon the real events of the voyage of the Missionaries, as given in Crantz's History. — See the Appendix, note (F).

Heaven in the vision of eternal bliss,
Death's terrors, hell's unsearchable abyss;
— Though rapt in secrecy from human eye,
These in the mind's profound sensorium lie,
And, with their Maker, by a glance of thought,
Are in a moment to remembrance brought;
Then most, when most restrain'd the' imperfect sight,
God and his works shine forth in His own light.
Yet clearest through that veil the Pilgrims trace
Their Father's image in their Saviour's face;
A sigh can waft them to his feet in prayer,
Not Gabriel bends with more acceptance there,
Nor to the throne from heaven's pure altar rise
The odors of a sweeter sacrifice,
Than when before the mercy-seat they kneel,
And tell Him all they fear, or hope, or feel;
Perils without, and enemies within,
Satan, the world, temptation, weakness, sin;
Yet rest unshaken on his sure defence,
Invincible through his omnipotence:
"Oh! step by step," they cry, "direct our way,
And give thy grace, like manna, day by day;
The store of yesterday will not suffice,
To-morrow's sun to us may never rise;
Safe only, when our souls are stay'd on Thee;
Rich only, when we know our poverty."

And step by step the Lord those suppliants led;
He gave them daily grace like daily bread;

By sea, on shore, through all their pilgrimage,
In rest and labor, to their latest age,
Sharp though their trials, and their comforts scant,
God was their refuge, and they knew not want.

On rustling pinions, like an unseen bird,
Among the yards, a stirring breeze is heard;
The conscious vessel wakes as from a trance,
Her colors float, the filling sails advance;
White from her prow the murmuring surge recedes:
— So the swan, startled from her nest of reeds,
Swells into beauty, and with curving chest,
Cleaves the blue lake, with motion soft as rest.
Light o'er the liquid lawn the pageant glides;
Her helm the well-experienced pilot guides,
And while he threads the mist-enveloped maze,
Turns to the magnet his inquiring gaze,
In whose mute oracle, where'er he steers,
The pointing hand of Providence appears;
With this, though months of gloom the main enrobe,
His keel might plough a furrow round the globe.

Again the night ascends without a star:
Low sounds come booming o'er the waves afar,
As if conflicting navies shook the flood,
With human thunders in the strife of blood,
That slay more victims in one brief campaign,
Than heaven's own bolts through centuries have slain.
The seaman hearkens; — color flies his cheek,
His stout heart throbs with fears he dare not speak.

No lightning-splendors streak the' unbroken gloom;
— His bark may shoot the gulf beyond the tomb,
And he, if e'er it come, may meet a light,
Which never yet hath dawn'd on living sight.
Fresher and fresher blows the' insurgent gale;
He reefs his tops, he narrows sail by sail,
Yet feels the ship with swifter impulse sweep
O'er mightier billows, the recoiling deep;
While still, with doleful omen on his ear,
Come the deep echoes of those sounds of fear,
Distant, — yet every volley rolls more near.

Oh! in that agony of thought forlorn,
How longs the' impatient mariner for morn!
She wakes, — his eyes are wither'd to behold
The scene which her disastrous beams unfold:
The fog is vanish'd, but the welkin lowers,
Sharp hail descends, and sleet in blinding showers;
Ocean one bed of foam, with fury tost,
In undistinguishable whiteness lost,
Save where vast fields of ice their surface show,
Buoyant, but many a fathom sunk below:
Changing his station as the fragments pass,
Death stands the pilot of each ponderous mass;
Gathering his brow into the darkest frown,
He bolts his raft to run the victim down,
But shoots astern: — the shock the vessel feels,
A moment in the giddy whirlpool reels,
Then like an arrow soars, as through the air,
So high the salient waves their burden bear.

Quick skirmishes with floating batteries past,
Ruin inevitable threats at last:
Athwart the north, like ships of battle spread,
Winter's flotilla, by their captain led,
(Who boasts with these to make his prowess known,
And plant his foot beyond the arctic zone,)
Islands of ice, so wedged and grappled lie,
One moving continent appals the eye,
And to the ear renews those notes of doom,
That brought portentous warnings through the gloom;
For loud and louder, with explosive shocks,
Sudden convulsions split the frost-bound rocks,
And launch loose mountains on the frothing ooze,
As pirate-barks, on summer seas to cruize.
In front this perilous array; — behind,
Borne on the surges, driven by the wind,
The vessel hurries to the brink of fate;
All efforts fail, — but prayer is not too late:
Then, in the imminent and ghastly fall
Foul on destruction, — the disciples call
On Him, their Master, who, in human form,
Slept in the lap of the devouring storm;
On Him, who in the midnight watch was seen,
Walking the gulf, ineffably serene,
At whose rebuke the tempest ceased to roar,
The winds caress'd the waves, the waves the shore.
On Him they call; — their prayer, in faith preferr'd
Amidst the frantic hurricane, is heard;
He gives the sign, by none in earth or heaven
Known, but by him to whom the charge is given,

The Angel of the Waters; — he, whose wrath
Had hurl'd the vessel on that shipwreck path,
Becomes a minister of grace; — his breath
Blows, — and the enemies are scatter'd, — Death,
Reft of his quarry, plunges through the wave,
Buried himself where he had mark'd their grave.
The line of battle broken, and the chain
Of that armada, which oppress'd the main,
Snapt hopelessly asunder, quickly all
The' enormous masses in disruption fall,
And the weak vessel, through the chaos wild,
Led by the mighty Angel, — as a child,
Snatch'd from its crib, and in the mother's arms
Borne through a midnight tumult of alarms, —
Escapes the wrecks; nor slackens her career,
Till sink the forms, and cease the sounds of fear,
And He, who rules the universe at will,
Saith to the reinless elements, "Be still."

Then rise sweet hymns of gratulation; praise
From hearts and voices, in harmonious lays; —
So Israel sang deliverance, when he stood
By the Red Sea, and saw the morning-flood,
That in its terrible embraces bore
The slain pursuers and their spoils on shore.

Light-breathing gales awhile their course propel,
The billows roll with pleasurable swell,
Till the seventh dawn; when o'er the pure expanse
The Sun, like lightning, throws his earliest glance,

"Land; Land!" exclaims the ship-boy from the mast,
"Land! Land!" with one electric shock hath pass'd
From lip to lip, and every eye hath caught
The cheering glimpse so long, so dearly sought;
Yet must imagination half supply
The doubtful streak, dividing sea and sky;
Nor clearly known, till in sublimer day,
From icy cliffs refracted splendors play,
And clouds of sea-fowl high in ether sweep,
Or fall like stars through sunshine on the deep.
'T is Greenland! but so desolately bare,
Amphibious life alone inhabits there;
'T is Greenland! yet so beautiful the sight,
The Brethren gaze with undisturb'd delight:
In silence (as before the Throne), they stand,
And pray, in prospect of that promised land,
That He, who sends them thither may abide
Through the waste howling wilderness their guide;
And the good shepherd seek his straying flocks,
Lost on those frozen waves and herbless rocks,
By the still waters of his comforts lead,
And in the pastures of salvation feed.

Their faith must yet be tried:— the sun at noon
Shrinks from the shadow of the passing moon,
Till, ray by ray of all his pomp bereft
(Save one slight ring of quivering lustre left),
Total eclipse involves his peerless eye:
Portentous twilight creeps around the sky;

The frighted sea-birds to their haunts repair;
There is a freezing stillness in the air,
As if the blood through Nature's veins ran cold,
A prodigy so fearful to behold;
A few faint stars gleam through the dread serene,
Trembling and pale spectators of the scene;
While the rude mariners, with stern amaze,
As on some tragic execution gaze,
When calm but awful guilt is stretcht to feel
The torturing fire, or dislocating wheel,
And life, like light from yonder orb, retires,
Spark after spark, till the whole man expires.
Yet may the darken'd sun and mourning skies
Point to a higher, holier sacrifice;
The Brethren's thoughts to Calvary's brow ascend,
Round the Redeemer's Cross their spirits bend,
And while heaven frowns, earth shudders, graves disclose
The forms of sleepers, startled from repose,
They catch the blessing of his latest breath,
Mark his last look, and through the' eclipse of death
See lovelier beams than Tabor's vision shed,
Wreathe a meek halo round his sacred head.
To Greenland then, with quick compassion, turn
Their deepest sympathies; their bosoms burn,
To her barbarian race, with tongues of flame,
His love, his grief, his glory to proclaim.

O could they view, in this alarming hour,
Those wretched ones, themselves beneath the power

Of darkness, while the shadow clips the sun!
How to their dens the fierce sea-hunters run,
Who death in every shape of peril brave,
By storms and monsters, on the faithless wave,
But now in speechless horror lie aghast,
Till the malignant prodigy be past:
While bolder females, with tormenting spells,
Consult their household dogs as oracles,
And by the yelping of their curs divine
That still the earth may stand, the sun may shine.
Then forth they creep, and to their offspring tell
What fate of old a youth and maid befell: *
How, in the age of night, ere day was born
On the blue hills of undiscover'd morn;
Where one pale cresset twinkled through the shade,
MALINA and her gay companions play'd
A thousand mimic sports, as children wont;
They hide, they seek, they shoot, harpoon and hunt;
When lo! ANINGA, passionate and young,
Keen as a wolf, upon his sister sprung,
And pounced his victim; — gentler way to woo
He knew not, or he scorn'd it if he knew:
MALINA snatch'd her lamp, and in the dark
Dash'd on his felon-front a hideous mark,
Slipt from his foul embrace (and laugh'd aloud),
Soft as the rainbow melting from the cloud;

* For the fable of Malina and Aninga (the Sun and the Moon), see note (G) of the Appendix; which also explains the allusions here made to the terror of the men, and the courage and spells of the women, during eclipses of the Sun.

Then shot to heaven, and in her wondrous flight
Transform'd her image, sparkled into light,
Became the sun, and through the firmament,
Forth in the glory of a goddess went.
ANINGA baffled, madden'd, unsubdued,
By her own beams the fugitive pursued,
And when she set, his broad disfigured mien
As the dim moon among the stars was seen;
Thenceforward doom'd his sister's steps to chase,
But ne'er o'ertake in heaven's eternal race.
Yet when his vanish'd orb might seem to sleep,
He takes his monthly pastime on the deep,
Through storms, o'er cataracts, in his Kayak sails,
Strikes with unerring dart the polar whales,
Or o'er ice-mountains, in his dog-drawn car,
Pursues the reindeer to the furthest star.
But when eclipse his baneful disk invades,
He prowls for prey among the Greenland maids,
Till roaring drums, belaboring sticks, and cries
Repel the errant Demon to the skies.

The sun hath cast aside his veil;—he shines
With purest splendor till his orb declines;
Then landward, marshalling in black array,
Eruptive vapors drive him from the day;
And night again, with premature control,
Binds light in chains of darkness o'er the pole;
Heaven in one ebon mass of horror scowls:
—Anon a universal whirlwind howls,

With such precipitation dash'd on high,
Not from one point, but from the whole dark sky,
The surges at the onset shrink aghast,
Borne down beneath the paralyzing blast;
But soon the mad tornado slants its course,
And rolls them into mountains by main force,
Then utterly embroil'd, through clouds and waves,
As 'twixt two oceans met in conflict, raves.
Now to the passive bark, alternate tost,
Above, below, both sea and sky are lost,
All but the giddy summit, where her keel
Hangs in light balance on the billowy wheel;
Then, as the swallow in his windward flight,
Quivers the wing, returns, and darts downright,
She plunges through the blind abyss, and o'er
Her groaning masts the cavern'd waters roar.
Ruled by the hurricane, no more the helm
Obeys the pilot; — seas on seas o'erwhelm
The deck; where oft embattled currents meet,
Foam in white whirlpools, flash to spray, retreat,
And rock the vessel with their huge turmoils,
Like the cork-float around the fisher's toils.
Three days of restless agony, that seem
Of one delirious night the waking dream,
The mariners in vain their labors ply,
Or sick at heart in pale despondence lie.
The Brethren weak, yet firm as when they faced
Winter's ice-legions on his own bleak waste,
In patient hope, that utters no complaint,
Pray without ceasing; pray, and never faint;

Assured that He, who from the tempest's neck
Hath loosed his grasp, still holds it at his beck,
And with a pulse too deep for mortal sense,
— The secret pulse of his omnipotence,
That beats through every motion of the storm,
— Can check destruction in its wildest form:
Bow'd to his will, — their lot how truly blest,
Who live to serve Him, and who die to rest!

To live and serve Him is their Lord's decree;
He curbs the wind, He calms the' infuriate sea;
The sea and wind their Maker's yoke obey,
And waft his servants on their destined way.
Though many a league by that disaster driven [riven,
'Thwart from their course; with planks and cordage
With hands disabled, and exhausted strength,
The active crew refit their bark at length;
Along the placid gulf, with heaving sails,
That catch from every point propitious gales,
Led like the moon, from infancy to age,
Round the wide zodiac of her pilgrimage,
Onward and smooth their voyage they pursue
Till Greenland's coast again salutes their view.

'T is sunset: to the firmament serene,
The' Atlantic wave reflects a gorgeous scene;
Broad in the cloudless west a belt of gold
Girds the blue hemisphere; above unroll'd
The keen, clear air grows palpable to sight,
Embodied in a flush of crimson light,

Through which the evening star, with milder gleam,
Descends, to meet her image in the stream.
Far in the east, what spectacle unknown
Allures the eye to gaze on it alone?
— Amidst black rocks, that lift on either hand
Their countless peaks, and mark receding land;
Amidst a tortuous labyrinth of seas,
That shine around the arctic Cyclades;
Amidst a coast of dreariest continent,
In many a shapeless promontory rent;
— O'er rocks, seas, islands, promontories spread,
The Ice-Blink rears its undulated head,*
On which the sun, beyond the' horizon shrined,
Hath left his richest garniture behind;
Piled on a hundred arches, ridge by ridge,
O'er fix'd and fluid strides the Alpine bridge,
Whose blocks of sapphire seem to mortal eye
Hewn from cerulean quarries of the sky;
With glacier-battlements, that crowd the spheres,
The slow creation of six thousand years,
Amidst immensity it towers sublime,
— Winter's eternal palace, built by Time:
All human structures by his touch are borne
Down to the dust; — mountains themselves are worn

* The term Ice-Blink is generally applied by our mariners to the nocturnal illumination in the heavens, which denotes to them the proximity of ice mountains. In this place a description is attempted of the most stupendous accumulation of ice in the known world, which has been long distinguished under this peculiar name by the Danish navigators.

With his light footsteps; *here* for ever grows,
Amid the region of unmelting snows,
A monument; where every flake that falls,
Gives adamantine firmness to the walls.
The sun beholds no mirror, in his race,
That shows a brighter image of his face;
The stars, in their nocturnal vigils, rest
Like signal fires on its illumined crest;
The gliding moon around the ramparts wheels,
And all its magic lights and shades reveals;
Beneath, the tide with idle fury raves
To undermine it through a thousand caves;
Rent from its roof, though thundering fragments oft
Plunge to the gulf; immovable aloft,
From age to age, in air, o'er sea, on land,
Its turrets heighten and its piers expand.

Midnight hath told his hour; the moon yet young,
Hangs in the argent west her bow unstrung;
Larger and fairer, as her lustre fades,
Sparkle the stars amidst the deepening shades:
Jewels more rich than night's regalia gem
The distant Ice-Blink's spangled diadem;
Like a new morn from orient darkness, there
Phosphoric splendors kindle in mid air,
As though from heaven's self-opening portals came
Legions of spirits in an orb of flame,
— Flame, that from every point an arrow sends,
Far as the concave firmament extends:

Spun with the tissue of a million lines,
Glistening like gossamer the welkin shines:
The constellations in their pride look pale
Through the quick trembling brilliance of that veil;
Then suddenly converged, the meteors rush
O'er the wide south; one deep vermilion blush
O'erspreads Orion glaring on the flood,
And rabid Sirius foams through fire and blood;
Again the circuit of the pole they range,
Motion and figure every moment change,
Through all the colors of the rainbow run,
Or blaze like wrecks of a dissolving sun;
Wide ether burns with glory, conflict, flight,
And the glad ocean dances in the light.

The seaman's jealous eye askance surveys
This pageantry of evanescent rays,
While in the horror of misgiving fear
New storms already thunder on his ear:
But morning comes, and brings him sweet release;
Day shines and sets; at evening all is peace;
Another and another day is past;
The fourth appears, — the loveliest and the last;
The sails are furl'd; the anchor drags the sand;
The boat hath cross'd the creek; — the Brethren land.

END OF CANTO III.

CANTO FOURTH.

Retrospect of ancient Greenland:— The Discovery of Iceland, of Greenland, of Wineland.— The Norwegian Colonies on the Eastern and Western Coasts of Greenland; the Appearance of the Skraellings, or modern Greenlanders, in the West, and the Destruction of the Norwegian Settlers in that Quarter.

HERE while in peace the weary Pilgrims rest,
Turn we our voyage from the new-found west,
Sail up the current of departed time,
And seek along its banks that vanish'd clime,
By ancient scalds in Runic verse renown'd,
Now like old Babylon no longer found.
—"Oft was I weary when I toil'd at thee;"*
This, on an oar abandon'd to the sea,
Some hand had graven:—From what founder'd boat
It fell;—how long on ocean's waves afloat;
—Who mark'd it with that melancholy line;
No record tells:—Greenland! such fate was thine;
Whate'er thou wast, of thee remains no more
Than a brief legend on a foundling oar;
And he, whose song would now revive thy fame,
Grasps but the shadow of a mighty name.

* About the middle of the seventeenth century, an oar was drifted on the coast of Iceland, bearing this inscription in Runic characters:—

"Oft var ek dasa, dur ek dro thik."

"Oft was I weary when I drew thee." This oar was conjectured to have been brought from East Greenland, a hundred and fifty years after the last ship sailed from Norway for that coast.

From Asia's fertile womb, when Time was young,
And earth a wreck, the sires of nations sprung;
In Shinar's land of rivers, Babel's tower
Stood the lorn relic of their scatter'd power;
A broken pillar, snapt as from the spheres,
Slow-wasting through the silent lapse of years,
While o'er the regions, by the flood destroy'd,
The builders breathed new life throughout the void,
Soul, passion, intellect; till blood of man
Through every artery of Nature ran;
O'er eastern islands pour'd its quickening stream,
Caught the warm crimson of the western beam,
Beneath the burning line made fountains start
In the dry wilderness of Afric's heart,
And through the torpid north, with genial heat,
Taught love's exhilarating pulse to beat;
Till the great sun, in his perennial round,
Man, of all climes the restless native, found,
Pursuing folly in his vain career,
As if existence were immortal here;
While on the fathers' graves the sons, untaught
By their mischance, the same illusions sought,
By gleams and shadows measured woe and bliss,
As though unborn for any world but this.

Five thousand years, unvisited, unknown,
Greenland lay slumbering in the frozen zone,—
While heaven's resplendent host pursued their way
To light the wolf and eagle to their prey,
And tempests o'er the main their terrors spread
To rock Leviathan upon his bed;—

Ere Ingolf his undaunted flag unfurl'd
To search the secrets of the polar world.*
'T was liberty, that fires the coldest veins,
And exile, famine, death, prefers to chains;
'T was liberty, through floods unploughed before,
That led his gallant crew from Norway's shore;
They cut their cable, and in thunder broke
With their departing oars the tyrant's yoke;
The deep their country, and their bark their home,
A floating isle, on which they joy'd to roam
Amidst immensity; with waves and wind,
Now sporting and now wrestling; — unconfined,
Save by the blue surrounding firmament,
Full, yet for ever widening as they went:
Thus sail'd those mariners, unheeding where
They found a port, if Freedom anchor'd there.

By stars that never set, their course they steer'd,
And northward with indignant impulse veer'd,
For sloth had lull'd, and luxury o'errun,
And bondage seized, the realms that loved the sun.

* Among numerous incoherent traditions, it is recorded that Iceland was first discovered by one Flokko, a pirate, who, being bewildered at sea, let fly (as was the custom of the Norwegians in such extremities) a raven, which, soaring to a great elevation, discerned land, and made for it. Flokko followed, and arriving at a mountainous coast covered with snow and glaciers, called it Iceland. Some time afterwards, about the year 874, Ingolf, a Norwegian earl, with his vassals, escaping from the tyranny of Harold Harfagar, pursued the same course as Flokko, and, by the same experiment with a raven, rediscovered Iceland; which he and his followers peopled, and there he established a commonwealth that reflected honor on an age of barbarism.

At length by mountain-ice, with perils strange,
Menaced, repell'd, and forced their track to change,
They bade the unimprison'd raven fly,
A living compass through the chartless sky:
Up to the zenith, swift as fire, he soar'd,
Through the clear boundless atmosphere explored
The dim horizon stretcht beneath his sight;
Then to the west full-onward shot his flight:
Thither they follow; till from Thule's rocks,
Around the bird of tempests rose the flocks
Of screaming sea-fowl, widening ring o'er ring,
Till heaven grew dark; then wheeling on the wing
Landward they whiten all the rocks below,
Or diving melt into the gulf like snow.
Pleased with the proud discovery, Ingolf gave
His lintel and his doorposts to the wave,
Divining as they drifted to the strand
The will of destiny, — the place to land.*
There on a homeless soil his foot he placed,
Framed his hut-palace, colonized the waste,
And ruled his horde with patriarchal sway;
— Where justice reigns, 't is freedom to obey:
And there his race, in long succession blest,
(Like generations in the eagle's nest,
Upon their own hereditary rock,)
Flourish'd, invincible to every shock

* This device of superstition is borrowed from the tradition concerning Ingolf, and probably the same was frequently employed by the northern rovers, leaving their native country, and seeking a home in strange lands.

Of time, chance, foreign force, or civil rage,—
A noble dynasty from age to age;
And Iceland shone for generous lore renown'd,
A northern light, when all was gloom around.

Ere long, by brave adventurers on the tide,
A new Hesperian region was descried,
Which fancy deem'd, or fable feign'd, so fair,
Fleets from old Norway pour'd their settlers there,
Who traced and peopled far that double shore,
Round whose repelling rocks two oceans roar,
Till at the southern promontory, tost
By tempests, each is in its rival lost.
Thus Greenland (so that arctic world they named)
Was planted, and to utmost Calpe famed
For wealth exhaustless, which her seas could boast,
And prodigies of Nature on her coast;
Where, in the green recess of every glen,
The House of Prayer o'ertopt the' abodes of men,
And flocks and cattle grazed by summer-streams,
That track'd the valleys with meandering gleams:
While on the mountains ice eternal frown'd,
And growing glaciers deepen'd tow'rds the ground,
Year after year, as centuries roll'd away,
Nor lost one moment till that judgment-day
When eastern Greenland from the world was rent,
Ingulf'd,—or fix'd one frozen continent.*

* The extravagant accounts of the fertility of ancient Greenland need not be particularized here. Some of the annals state, that the best wheat grew to perfection in the valleys; that the

'T were long and dreary to recount in rhyme
The crude traditions of that long-lost clime:
To sing of wars, by barbarous chieftains waged,
In which as fierce and noble passions raged,
Heroes as subtle, bold, remorseless, fought,
And deeds as dark and terrible were wrought,
As round Troy-walls, became the splendid themes
Of Homer's song, and Jove's Olympian dreams;
When giant-prowess, in the iron field,
With single arm made phalanx'd legions yield;
When battle was but massacre, — the strife
Of murderers, — steel to steel, and life to life.
— Who follows Homer takes the field too late;
Though stout as Hector, sure of Hector's fate,
A wound as from Achilles' spear he feels,
Falls, and adorns the Grecian's chariot-wheels.

Nor stay we monkish legends to rehearse;
To build their cloister-walls in Gothic verse;
Of groves and gardens, wine and music tell;
Fresh roses breathing round the hermit's cell,
And baths, in which Diana's nymphs might lave,
— From earth's self-opening veins the blood-warm
 wave,

forests were extensive and luxuriant; flocks and herds were numerous, and very large and fat, etc. At St. Thomas's Cloister, there was a natural fountain of hot water (a *geyser*), which, being conveyed by pipes into all the apartments of the monks, ministered to their comfort in many ways. Adjoining this cloister there was a richly cultivated garden, through which a warm rivulet flowed, and rendered the soil so fertile, that it produced the most beautiful flowers and the most delicious fruits.

Whose genial streams, amidst disparted ice,
Made laps of verdure, — like those isles of spice
In eastern seas; or rich oases, graced
With flowers and fountains, in the Libyan waste.

Rather the muse would stretch a mightier wing,
Of a new world the earliest dawn to sing;
How, — long ere Science, in a dream of thought,
Earth's younger daughter to Columbus brought,
And sent him, like the Faerie Prince, in quest
Of *that* " bright vestal throned in the west." *
— Greenland's bold sons, by instinct, sallied forth
On barks, like icebergs drifting from the north,
Cross'd without magnet undiscover'd seas,
And, all surrendering to the stream and breeze,
Touch'd on the line of that twin-bodied land,
That stretches forth to either pole a hand,
From arctic wilds that see no winter-sun,
To where the oceans of the world are one,
And round Magellan's streights, Fuego's shore,
Atlantic, Indian, and Pacific roar.

Regions of beauty there these rovers found,
The flowery hills with emerald woods were crown'd;

* Spenser introduces Prince Arthur as traversing the world in search of his mistress Gloriana, whom he had only seen in a dream. The discovery of a region in the west, by the Greenland Norwegians, about the year 1000, and intercourse maintained with it for 120 years afterwards, may be considered as the most curious fact or fable connected with the history of these colonists. The reason why it was called *Wineland*, is given in the sequel. — See also note (H) in the Appendix.

Spread o'er the vast savannahs, buffalo herds
Ranged without master; and the bright-wing'd birds
Made gay the sunshine as they glanced along,
Or turn'd the air to music with their song.

Here from his mates a German youth had stray'd,
Where the broad river cleft the forest glade;
Swarming with alligator-shoals, the flood
Blazed in the sun, or moved in clouds of blood;
The wild boar rustled headlong through the brake;
Like a live arrow leap'd the rattle-snake;
The uncouth shadow of the climbing bear
Crawl'd on the grass, while he aspired in air;
Anon with hoofs, like hail, the greenwood rang,
Among the scattering deer a panther sprang:
The stripling fear'd not, — yet he trod with awe,
As if enchantment breathed o'er all he saw,
Till in his path uprose a wilding vine;
— Then o'er his memory rush'd the noble Rhine;
Home and its joys, with fulness of delight,
So rapt his spirit, so beguiled his sight,
That, in those glens of savage solitude,
Vineyards and corn-fields, towns and spires he view'd,
And through the image-chamber of his soul
The days of other years like shadows stole;
All that he once had been, again he grew,
Through every stage of life he pass'd anew;
The playmates of his infancy were there,
With dimpled cheeks, blue eyes, and flaxen hair;

The blithe companions of his riper youth,
And one whose heart was love, whose soul was truth.
— When the quick-mingling pictures of that dream
(Like broken scenery on a troubled stream,
Where sky and landscape, light and darkness, run
Through widening circles,) harmonized in one,
His father's cot appear'd, with vine-leaves drest,
And clusters pendent round the swallow's nest;
In front the little garden, at whose gate,
Amidst their progeny, his parents sate,
He only absent; — but his mother's eye
Look'd through a tear; — she reach'd him with a sigh:
Then in a moment vanish'd time and space,
And with a shout he rush'd to her embrace;
Round hills and dales the joyful tidings spread,
All ran to welcome Tyrker from the dead.
With bliss inebriate, in that giddy trance,
He led his waltzing partner through the dance;
And while he pluck'd the grapes that blush'd at hand,
Trod the rich wine-press in his native land,
Quaff'd the full flowing goblet, loosed his tongue,
And songs of vintage, harvest, battle sung,
At length his shipmates came: their laughter broke
The gay delusion; in alarm he 'woke:
Transport to silent melancholy changed;
At once from love, and joy, and hope estranged,
O'er his blank mind, with cold bereaving spell,
Came that heart-sickness which no tongue can tell;

— Felt when, in foreign climes, 'midst sounds unknown,
We hear the speech or music of our own,
Roused to delight, from drear abstraction start,
And feel our country beating at our heart;
The rapture of a moment; — in its birth
It perishes for ever from the earth;
And dumb, like shipwreck'd mariners we stand,
Eyeing by turns the ocean and the land,
Breathless; — till tears the struggling thought release,
And the lorn spirit weeps itself to peace.

Wineland the glad discoverers call'd that shore,
And back the tidings of its riches bore;
But soon return'd with colonizing bands,
— Men that at home would sigh for unknown lands;
Men of all weathers, fit for every toil,
War, commerce, pastime, peace, adventure, spoil;
Bold master-spirits, where they touch'd they gain'd
Ascendance; where they fix'd their foot they reign'd.
Both coasts they long inherited, though wide
Dissever'd; stemming to and fro the tide,
Free as the Syrian dove explores the sky,
Their helm their hope, their compass in their eye,
They found at will, where'er they pleased to roam,
The ports of strangers or their northern home,
Still 'midst tempestuous seas and zones of ice,
Loved as their own, their *unlost* Paradise.
— Yet was their Paradise forever lost:
War, famine, pestilence, the power of frost,

Their woes combining, wither'd from the earth
This late creation, like a timeless birth,
The fruit of age and weakness, forced to light,
Breathing awhile, — relapsing into night.

Ages had seen the vigorous race, that sprung
From Norway's stormy forelands, rock'd when young
In ocean's cradle, hardening as they rose,
Like mountain-pines amidst perennial snows;
— Ages had seen these sturdiest sons of Time
Strike root and flourish in that ruffian clime,
Commerce with lovelier lands and wealthier hold,
Yet spurn the lures of luxury and gold;
Beneath the umbrage of the Gallic vine,
For moonlight snows and cavern-shelter pine;
Turn from Campanian fields a lofty eye
To gaze upon the glorious Alps, and sigh,
Remembering Greenland; more and more endear'd,
As far and further from its shores they steer'd;
Greenland their world, — and all was strange beside;
Elsewhere they wander'd: here they lived and died.

At length a swarthy tribe, without a name,
Unknown the point of windward whence they came;
The power by which stupendous gulfs they cross'd,
Or compass'd wilds of everlasting frost,
Alike mysterious; — found their sudden way
To Greenland; pour'd along the western bay
Their straggling families; and seized the soil
For their domain, the ocean for their spoil.

Skraellings the Normans call'd these hordes in scorn,
That seem'd created on the spot, — though born
In trans-Atlantic climes, and thither brought
By paths as covert as the birth of thought;
They were at once; — the swallow-tribes in spring
Thus daily multiply upon the wing,
As if the air, their element of flight,
Brought forth new broods from darkness every night;
Slipt from the secret hand of Providence,
They come we see not how, nor know we whence.*

A stunted, stern, uncouth, amphibious stock,
Hewn from the living marble of the rock,
Or sprung from mermaids, and in ocean's bed,
With orcs and seals, in sunless caverns bred,
They might have held, from unrecorded time,
Sole patrimony in that hideous clime,
So lithe their limbs, so fenced their frames to bear
The intensest rigors of the polar air;
Nimble, and muscular, and keen to run
The rein-deer down a circuit of the sun;
To climb the slippery cliffs, explore their cells,
And storm and sack the sea-birds' citadels;
In bands, through snows, the mother-bear to trace,
Slay with their darts the cubs in her embrace,
And, while she lick'd their bleeding wounds, to brave
Her deadliest vengeance in her inmost cave:

* See note (I) of the Appendix.

Train'd with inimitable skill to float,
Each, balanced in his bubble of a boat,
With dexterous paddle steering through the spray,
With poised harpoon to strike his plunging prey,
As though the skiff, the seaman, oar, and dart
Were one compacted body, by one heart
With instinct, motion, pulse, empower'd to ride
A human Nautilus upon the tide;
Or with a fleet of Kayaks to assail
The desperation of the stranded whale,
When wedged 'twixt jagged rocks he writhes and rolls
In agony among the ebbing shoals,
Lashing the waves to foam, until the flood,
From wounds, like geysers, seems a bath of blood,
Echo all night dumb-pealing to his roar,
Till morn beholds him slain along the shore.

Of these, — hereafter should the lyre be strung
To arctic themes, — may glorious days be sung;
Now be our task the sad reverse to tell,
How in their march the nobler Normans fell; *

* The incidents alluded to in this clause are presumed to have occasioned the extinction of the Norwegian colonists on the western coast of Greenland. Crantz says, that there is a district on Ball's river, called Pissiksarbik, or the *place of arrows;* where it is believed, that the Skraellings and Norwegians fought a battle, in which the latter were defeated. The modern Greenlanders affirm, that the name is derived from the circumstance of the parties having shot their arrows at one another from opposite banks of the stream. Many *rudera*, or ruins of ancient buildings, principally supposed to have been churches, are found along the coast from Disko Bay to Cape Farewell.

— Whether by dire disease, that turn'd the breath
Of bounteous heaven to pestilence and death,
In number, strength, and spirit worn away,
Their lives became the cool assassin's prey;
— Or in the battle-field, as Skraellings boast,
These pigmies put to flight their giant-host,
When front to front on scowling cliffs they stood,
And shot their barbs athwart the parting flood;
Arrow smote arrow, dart encounter'd dart,
From hand to hand, impaling heart for heart;
Till spent their missiles: quick as in a dream
The images are changed; across the stream
The Skraellings rush'd, the precipices scaled;
— O'erwhelm'd by multitudes, the Normans fail'd:
A scatter'd remnant to the south retired,
But one by one along their route expired:
They perish'd; — History can no more relate
Of their obscure and unlamented fate:
They perish'd; — yet along that western shore,
Where Commerce spread her colonies of yore,
Ruins of temples and of homes are traced,
— Steps of magnificence amidst the waste
Where Time hath trod, and left those wrecks to show
That Life hath been, where all is death below.

END OF CANTO IV.

CANTO FIFTH.

The Depopulation of the Norwegian Colonies on the Eastern Coast of Greenland, and the Abandonment of Intercourse with it from Europe, in consequence of the Increase of the Arctic Ices about the beginning of the Fifteenth Century.

LAUNCH on the gulf, my little Greenland bark!
Bear me through scenes unutterably dark;
Scenes with the mystery of Nature seal'd,
Nor till the day of doom to be reveal'd.
What though the spirits of the arctic gales
Freeze round thy prow, or fight against thy sails,
Safe as Arion, whom the dolphin bore,
Enamor'd of his music, to the shore,
On thee adventuring o'er an unknown main,
I raise to warring elements a strain
Of kindred harmony: — O, lend your breath,
Ye tempests! while I sing this reign of death:
Utter dark sayings of the days of old;
In parables upon my harp unfold
Deeds perish'd from remembrance; truth, array'd,
Like heaven by night, in emblematic shade,
When shines the horoscope, and star on star,
By what they are not lead to what they are;
Atoms, that twinkle in an infant's eye,
Are worlds, suns, systems in the' unbounded sky:
Thus the few fabled woes my strains create
Are hieroglyphics in a book of Fate;

And while the shadowy symbols I unroll,
Imagination reads a direr scroll.
Wake, ye wild visions! o'er the northern deep,
On clouds and winds, like warrior-spectres sweep;
Show by what plagues and hurricanes destroy'd,
A breathing realm became a torpid void.

The floods are raging, and the gales blow high,
Low as a dungeon-roof impends the sky;
Prisoners of hope, between the clouds and waves,
Six fearless sailors man yon boat, that braves
Peril redoubling upon peril past:
From childhood nurslings of the wayward blast,
Aloft as o'er a buoyant arch they go,
Whose keystone breaks; — as deep they plunge below;
Unyielding, though the strength of man be vain;
Struggling, though borne like surf along the main;
In front a battlement of rocks; in rear,
Billow on billow bounding: near, more near,
They verge to ruin; — life and death depend
On the next impulse; — shrieks and prayers ascend;
When, like the fish that mounts on drizzling wings,
Sheer from the gulf the' ejected vessel springs,
And grounds on inland ice, beyond the track
Of hissing foam-wreaths, whence the tide roll'd back;
Then ere that tide, returning to the charge,
Swallows the wreck, the captives are at large.
On either hand steep hills obstruct their path;
Behind, the ocean roaring in his wrath,

Mad as a Libyan wilderness by night,
With all its lions up, in chase or fight.
The fugitives right onward shun the beach,
Nor tarry till the inmost cove they reach,
Secluded in the labyrinthine dell,
Like the last hollow of a spiral shell.
There, with the axe or knife which haste could save,
They build a house; — perhaps they dig a grave:
Of solid snow, well-squared, and piled in blocks,
Brilliant as hewn from alabaster rocks,
Their palace rises, narrowing to the roof,
And freezes into marble, tempest-proof;
Night closing round, within its shade they creep,
And weary Nature sinks at once to sleep.

Oh! could we walk amidst their dreams, and see
All that they have been, are, or wish to be,
In fancy's world! — each at his own fire-side:
One greets a parent; one a new-made bride;
Another clasps his babe with fond embrace,
A smile in slumber mantling o'er his face;
All dangers are forgotten in a kiss,
Or but remember'd to exalt the bliss.
— One wounded sufferer wakes, with pain opprest,
Yet are his thoughts at home among the rest;
Then beams his eye, his heart dilated burns,
Till the dark vigil to a vision turns,
That vision to reality: and home
Is so endear'd, he vows no more to roam.
Ha! suddenly he starts: with trembling lips,
Salt shower drops, oozing through the roof, he sips:

Aware that instant, yet alarm'd too late,
— The sea hath burst its barrier, fix'd their fate;
Escape impossible: the tempests urge
Through the deep dell the inundating surge:
Nor wall nor roof the' impetuous flood controls;
Above, around, within, the deluge rolls:
He calls his comrades; — ere their doom be known,
'T is past; — the snow-house utterly o'erthrown,
Its inmates vanish; never to be found,
Living or dead, on habitable ground.

There is a beauteous hamlet in the vale;
Green are the fields around it; sweetly sail
The twilight shadows o'er the darkening scene,
Earth, air, and ocean, all alike serene;
Dipt in the hues of sunset, wreath'd in zones,
The clouds are resting on their mountain-thrones;
One peak alone exalts its glacier crest,
A golden paradise, above the rest;
Thither the day with lingering steps retires,
And in its own blue element expires:
Thus Aaron laid his gorgeous robes aside
On Horeb's consecrated top, and died.
The moon, meanwhile, o'er ocean's sombre bed,
New-risen, a thousand glow-worm lights hath spread;
From east to west the wildfire splendors glance,
And all the billows in her glory dance;
Till, in mid-heaven, her orb might seem the eye
Of Providence, wide-watching from the sky,
While Nature slumbers; — emblem of *His* grace
Whose presence fills the infinite of space.

The clouds have left the mountains; coldly bright,
Their icy summits shed cerulean light;
The steep declivities between assume
A horror of unfathomable gloom:
The village sleeps;—from house to house, the ear
Of yonder sentinel no sound can hear:
A maniac;—he, while calmer heads repose,
Takes his night round, to tell the stars his woes;
Woes, which his noble heart to frenzy stung;
—*He* hath no bard, and *they* remain unsung.
A warrior once, victorious arms he bore,
And bears them still, although his wars are o'er;
For 't is his boast, with shield and sword in hand,
To be the guardian Angel of the land.
Mark with what stern solemnity he stalks,
And to himself as to a legion talks:
Now deep in council with his chiefs; anon
He starts, as at the trumpet; leads them on,
And wins the day;—his battle-shout alarms
None but the infant in the nurse's arms;
Soon hush'd, but closer to her side, it sleeps;
While he abroad his watch in silence keeps.

At every door he halts, and brings a sigh,
But leaves a blessing, when he marches by:
He stops; from that low roof, a deadly groan
Hath made unutterable anguish known;
A spirit into eternity hath pass'd;
A spouse, a father, there hath breathed his last.
The widow and her little ones weep *not;*
In its excess their misery is forgot,

One dumb, dark moment; — then from all their eyes
Rain the salt tears, and loud their wailings rise:
Ah! little think that family forlorn
How brief the parting; — they shall meet ere morn!
For lo! the witness of their pangs hath caught
A sight that startles madness into thought:
Back from their gate unconsciously he reels;
A resurrection of his soul he feels.
There is a motion in the air: his eye
Blinks as it fear'd the falling of the sky.
The splendid peak of adamantine ice,
At sunset like an earthly paradise,
And in the moon of such empyrean hue,
It seem'd to bring the unseen world to view:
— That splendid peak, the Power (which to the spheres
Had piled its turrets through a thousand years)
Touches, as lightly as the passing wind,
And the huge mass, o'erbalanced, undermined,
And dislocated from its base of snow,
Slides down the slope, majestically slow,
Till o'er the precipice, down headlong sent,
And in ten thousand thousand spangles rent,
It piles a hill where spread a vale before:
— From rock to rock the echoes round the shore
Tell with their deep artillery the fate
Of the whole village crush'd beneath its weight.
— The sleepers wake, — their homes in ruins hurl'd,—
They wake — from death into another world.
The gazing maniac, palsied into stone,
Amidst the wreck of ice, survives alone;

A sudden interval of reason gleams,
Steady and clear, amidst his wildering dreams,
But shows reality in such a shape,
'T were rapture back to frenzy to escape.
Again the clouds of desolation roll,
Blotting all old remembrance from his soul:
Whate'er his sorrows or his joys have been,
His spirit grows embodied through *this* scene;
With eyes of agony, and clenching hands,
Fix'd in recoil, a frozen form he stands,
And, smit with wonder at his people's doom,
Becomes the monument upon their tomb.

Behold a scene, magnificent and new;
Nor land nor water meet the' excursive view;
The round horizon girds one frozen plain,
The mighty tombstone of the buried main,
Where, dark and silent, and unfelt to flow,
A dead sea sleeps with all its tribes below.
But heaven is still itself; the deep blue sky
Comes down with smiles to meet the glancing eye,
Though if a keener sight its bound would trace,
The arch recedes through everlasting space.
The sun, in morning glory, mounts his throne,
Nor shines he here in solitude unknown;
North, south, and west, by dogs or reindeer drawn,
Careering sledges cross the unbroken lawn,
And bring from bays and forelands round the coast,
Youth, beauty, valor, Greenland's proudest boast,
Who thus, in winter's long and social reign,
Hold feasts and tournaments upon the main,

When, built of solid floods, his bridge extends
A highway o'er the gulf to meeting friends,
Whom rocks impassable, or winds and tide,
Fickle and false, in summer months divide.

The scene runs round with motion, rings with mirth,
— No happier spot upon the peopled earth;
The drifted snow to dust the travellers beat,
The' uneven ice is flint beneath their feet.
Here tents, a gay encampment rise around,
Where music, song, and revelry resound;
There the blue smoke upwreathes a hundred spires,
Where humbler groups have lit their pine-wood fires.
Ere long they quit the tables; knights and dames
Lead the blithe multitude to boisterous games.
Bears, wolves, and lynxes yonder head the chase;
Here start the harness'd reindeer in the race;
Borne without wheels, a flight of rival cars
Track the ice-firmament, like shooting stars,
Right to the goal, converging as they run,
They dwindle through the distance into one.
Where smoother waves have form'd a sea of glass,
With pantomimic change the skaters pass; [wheel
Now toil like ships 'gainst wind and stream; then
Like flames blown suddenly asunder; reel
Like drunkards; then dispersed in tangents wide,
Away with speed invisible they glide.
Peace in their hearts, death-weapons in their hands,
Fierce in mock-battle meet fraternal bands,

Whom the same chiefs erewhile to conflict led,
When friends by friends, by kindred kindred bled.
Here youthful rings with pipe and drum advance,
And foot the mazes of the giddy dance;
Grey-beard spectators, with illumined eye,
Lean on their staves, and talk of days gone by;
Children, who mimic all, from pipe and drum
To chase and battle, dream of years to come.
Those years to come the young shall ne'er behold;
The days gone by no more rejoice the old.

There is a boy, a solitary boy,
Who takes no part in all this whirl of joy,
Yet, in the speechless transport of his soul,
He lives, and moves, and breathes throughout the whole:
Him should destruction spare, the plot of earth,
That forms his play-ground, gave a poet birth,
Who, on the wings of his immortal lays,
Thine heroes, Greenland! to the stars shall raise.
It must not be: — abruptly from the show
He turns his eyes; his thoughts are gone below
To sound the depths of ocean, where his mind
Creates the wonders which it cannot find.
Listening, as oft he listens in a shell
To the mock tide's alternate fall and swell,
He kneels upon the ice, — inclines his ear,
And hears, — or does he only seem to hear? —
A sound, as though the Genius of the deep
Heaved a long sigh, awaking out of sleep.

He starts; — 't was but a pulse within his brain!
No; — for he feels it beat through every vein;
Groan following groan, (as from a giant's breast,
Beneath a burying mountain, ill at rest,)
With awe ineffable his spirit thrills,
And rapture fires his blood, while terror chills.
The keen expression of his eye alarms
His mother; she hath caught him in her arms,
And learn'd the cause; — that cause, no sooner known,
From lip to lip, o'er many a league is flown;
Voices to voices, prompt as signals, rise
In shrieks of consternation to the skies:
Those skies, meanwhile, with gathering darkness scowl;
Hollow and winterly the bleak winds howl.
— From morn till noon had ether smiled serene,
Save one black-belted cloud, far eastward seen,
Like a snow-mountain; — there in ambush lay
The' undreaded tempest, panting for his prey:
That cloud by stealth hath through the welkin spread,
And hangs in meteor-twilight over-head;
At foot, beneath the adamantine floor,
Loose in their prison-house the surges roar:
To every eye, ear, heart, the' alarm is given,
And landward crowds, (like flocks of sea-fowl driven,
When storms are on the wing,) in wild affright,
On foot, in sledges, urge their panic flight,
In hope the refuge of the shore to gain
Ere the disruption of the struggling main,
Foretold by many a stroke, like lightning sent
In thunder, through the' unstable continent,

Which now, elastic on the swell below,
Rolls high in undulation to and fro.
Men, reindeer, dogs, the giddy impulse feel,
And, jostling headlong, back and forward reel:
While snow, sleet, hail, or whirling gusts of wind,
Exhaust, bewilder, stop the breath, and blind.
All is dismay and uproar; some have found
Death for deliverance, as they leap'd on ground,
Swept back into the flood: — but hope is vain:
Ere half the fugitives the beach can gain,
The fix'd ice, severing from the shore, with shocks
Of earthquake violence, bounds against the rocks;
Then suddenly, while on the verge they stand,
The whole recoils for ever from the land,
And leaves a gulf of foam along the shore,
In which whoever plunge are seen no more.

Ocean, meanwhile, abroad hath burst the roof
That sepulchred his waves; he bounds aloof.
In boiling cataracts, as volcanoes spout
Their fiery fountains, gush the waters out;
The frame of ice with dire explosion rends,
And down the' abyss the mingled crowd descends.
Heaven! from this closing horror hide thy light;
Cast thy thick mantle o'er it, gracious Night!
These screams of mothers with their infants lost,
These groans of agony from wretches tost
On rocks and whirlpools, — in thy storms be drown'd,
The crash of mountain-ice to atoms ground,
And rage of elements! — while winds, that yell
Like demons, peal the universal knell,

The shrouding waves around their limbs shall spread,
"And Darkness be the burier of the dead."
Their pangs are o'er: — at morn the tempests cease,
And the freed ocean rolls himself to peace;
Broad to the sun his heaving breast expands,
He holds his mirror to a hundred lands;
While cheering gales pursue the eager chase
Of billows round immeasurable space.*

Where are the multitudes of yesterday?
At morn they came; at eve they pass'd away.
Yet some survive; — yon castellated pile
Floats on the surges, like a fairy isle;
Preëminent upon its peak, behold,
With walls of amethyst and roofs of gold,
The semblance of a city; towers and spires
Glance in the firmament with opal fires:
Prone from those heights pellucid fountains flow
O'er pearly meads, through emerald vales below.
No lovelier pageant moves beneath the sky,†
Nor one so mournful to the nearer eye;

* The principal phenomena described in this disruption of so immense a breadth of ice, are introduced on the authority of an authentic narrative of a journey on sledges along the coast of Labrador, by two Moravian missionaries and a number of Esquimaux, in the year 1782. The first incident in this canto, the destruction of the snow house, is partly borrowed from the same record.

† The ice-bergs, both fixed and floating, present the most fantastic and magnificent forms, which an active imagination may easily convert into landscape scenery. Crantz says, that some of these look like churches, with pillars, arches, portals,

Here, when the bitterness of death had pass'd
O'er others, with their sledge and reindeer cast,
Five wretched ones, in dumb despondence wait
The lingering issue of a nameless fate;
A bridal party: — mark yon reverend sage
In the brown vigor of autumnal age;
His daughter in her prime; the youth, who won
Her love by miracles of prowess done;
With these, two meet companions of their joy,
Her younger sister, and a gallant boy,
Who hoped, like *him*, a gentle heart to gain
By valorous enterprise on land or main.
— These, when the ocean-pavement fail'd their feet,
Sought on a glacier's crags a safe retreat;
But in the shock, from its foundation torn,
That mass is slowly o'er the waters borne,
An ice-berg! — on whose verge all day they stand,
And eye the blank horizon's ring for land.
All night around a dismal flame they weep;
Their sledge, by piecemeal, lights the hoary deep.
Morn brings no comfort; at her dawn expire
The latest embers of their latest fire;
For warmth and food the patient reindeer bleeds,
Happier in death than those he warms and feeds.

and illuminated windows; others like castles, with square and spiral turrets. A third class assumes the appearance of ships in full sail, to which pilots have occasionally gone out, for the purpose of conducting them into harbor; many again resemble large islands, with hill and dale, as well as villages, and even cities, built upon the margin of the sea. Two of these stood for many years in Disco Bay, which the Dutch whalers called Amsterdam and Haarlem.

— How long, by that precarious raft upbuoy'd,
They blindly drifted on a shoreless void;
How long they suffer'd, or how soon they found
Rest in the gulf, or peace on living ground;
— Whether, by hunger, cold, and grief consumed,
They perish'd miserably — and unentomb'd
(While on that frigid bier their corses lay),
Became the sea-fowl's or the sea-bear's prey;
— Whether the wasting mound, by swift degrees,
Exhaled in mist and vanish'd from the seas,
While they, too weak to struggle even in death,
Lock'd in each other's arms resign'd their breath,
And their white skeletons, beneath the wave,
Lie intertwined in one sepulchral cave;
— Or meeting some Norwegian bark at sea,
They deem'd its deck a world of liberty;
Or sunward sailing, on green Erin's sod,
They kneel'd and worshipp'd a delivering God,
Where yet the blood they brought from Greenland runs
Among the noblest of our sister's sons,
— Is all unknown: — their ice-berg disappears
Amidst the flood of unreturning years.

Ages are fled; and Greenland's hour draws nigh;
Seal'd is the judgment; all her race must die;
Commerce forsakes the' unvoyageable seas,
That year by year with keener rigor freeze;
The' embargoed waves in narrower channels roll
To blue Spitzbergen and the utmost pole;

A hundred colonies, erewhile that lay
On the green marge of many a shelter'd bay,
Lapse to the wilderness; their tenants throng
Where streams in summer, turbulent and strong,
With molten ice from inland Alps supplied,
Hold free communion with the breathing tide,
That from the heart of ocean sends the flood
Of living water round the world, like blood;
But Greenland's pulse shall slow and slower beat,
Till the last spark of genial warmth retreat,
And, like a palsied limb of Nature's frame,
Greenland be nothing but a place and name.
That crisis comes; the wafted fuel fails; *
The cattle perish; famine long prevails;
With torpid sloth, intenser seasons bind
The strength of muscle and the spring of mind;
Man droops, his spirits waste, his powers decay,
— His generation soon shall pass away.

At moonless midnight, on this naked coast,
How beautiful in heaven the starry host!

* Greenland has been supplied with fuel, from time immemorial, brought by the tide from the northern shores of Asia, and other regions, probably even from California, and the coast of America towards Behring's Straits. This annual provision, however, has gradually been decreasing for some years past (being partly intercepted by the accumulation of ice) on the shores of *modern* Greenland, towards Davis's Straits. Should it fail altogether, that country (like the east) must become uninhabitable; as the natives themselves employ wood in the construction of their houses, their boats, and their implements of fishing, hunting, and shooting, and could not find any adequate substitute for it at home.

With lambent brilliance o'er these cloister-walls,
Slant from the firmament a meteor falls;
A steadier flame from yonder beacon streams,
To light the vessel, seen in golden dreams
By many a pining wretch, whose slumbers feign
The bliss for which he looks at morn in vain.
Two years are gone, and half expired a third
(The nation's heart is sick with hope deferr'd),
Since last for Europe sail'd a Greenland prow,
Her whole marine, — so shorn is Greenland now,
Though once, like clouds in ether unconfined,
Her naval wings were spread to every wind.
The monk, who sits, the weary hours to count,
In the lone block-house on the beacon-mount,
Watching the east, beholds the morning star
Eclipsed at rising o'er the waves afar,
As if — for so would fond expectance think —
A sail had cross'd it on the' horizon's brink.
His fervent soul in ecstasy outdrawn,
Glows with the shadows kindling through the dawn,
Till every bird that flashes through the brine
Appears an arm'd and gallant brigantine;
And every sound along the air that comes,
The voice of clarions and the roll of drums.
— 'T is she! 't is she! the well-known keel at last,
With Greenland's banner streaming at the mast;
The full-swoln sails, the spring-tide, and the breeze,
Waft on her way the pilgrim of the seas.
The monks at matins issuing from their cells,
Spread the glad tidings; while their convent-bells

Wake town and country, sea and shore, to bliss
Unknown for years on any morn but this.
Men, women, children throng the joyous strand,
Whose mob of moving shadows o'er the sand
Lengthen to giants, while the hovering sun
Lights up a thousand radiant points from one.
The pilots launch their boats: — a race! a race!
The strife of oars is seen in every face;
Arm against arm puts forth its might to reach,
And guide the welcome stranger to the beach.
— Shouts from the shore, the cliffs, the boats, arise;
No voice, no signal from the ship replies;
Nor on the deck, the yards, the bow, the stern,
Can keenest eye a human form discern.
Oh! that those eyes were open'd, there to see,
How, in serene and dreadful majesty,
Sits the destroying Angel at the helm!
— He, who hath lately march'd from realm to realm,
And from the palace to the peasant's shed,
Made all the living kindred to the dead:
Nor man alone, dumb nature felt his wrath,
Drought, mildew, murrain, strew'd his carnage-path;
Harvest and vintage cast their timeless fruit,
Forests before him wither'd from the root.
To Greenland now, with unexhausted power,
He comes commission'd; and in evil hour
Propitious elements prepare his way;
His day of landing is a festal day.

A boat arrives; — to those who scale the deck,
Of life appears but one disastrous wreck;

Fall'n from the rudder, which he feign had grasp'd,
But stronger Death his wrestling hold unclasp'd,
The film of darkness freezing o'er his eyes,
A lukewarm corpse, the brave commander lies;
Survivor sole of all his buried crew,
Whom one by one the rife contagion slew,
Just when the cliffs of Greenland cheer'd his sight,
Even from their pinnacle his soul took flight.
Chill'd at the spectacle, the pilots gaze
One on another, lost in blank amaze;
But from approaching boats, when rivals throng,
They seize the helm, in silence steer along,
And cast their anchor, 'midst exulting cries,
That make the rocks the echoes of the skies,
Till the mysterious signs of woes to come,
Circled by whispers, strike the uproar dumb.
Rumor affirms, that by some heinous spell
Of Lapland witches, crew and captain fell;
None guess the secret of perfidious fate,
Which all shall know too soon, — yet know too late.

The monks, who claim the ship, divide the stores
Of food and raiment at their convent-doors.
— A mother, hastening to her cheerless shed,
Breaks to her little ones untasted bread;
Clamorous as nestling birds, the hungry band
Receive a mortal portion at her hand:
On each would equal love the best confer,
Each by distinct affection dear to her;

One the first pledge that to her spouse she gave,
One unborn till he was in his grave;
This was *his* darling, that to *her* most kind;
A fifth was once a twin, the sixth is blind:
In each she lives; — in each by turns she dies;
Smitten by pestilence before her eyes,
Three days, and all are slain; — the heaviest doom
Is hers; their ice-barr'd cottage is their tomb.
— The wretch, whose limbs are impotent with cold,
In the warm comfort of a mantle roll'd,
Lies down to slumber on his soul's desire;
But wakes at morn, as wrapt in flames of fire:
Not Hercules, when from his breast he tore
The cloak envenom'd with the Centaur's gore,
Felt sharper pangs than he, who, mad with rage,
Dives in the gulf, or rolls in snow to' assuage
His quenchless agony; the rankling dart
Within him burns till it consumes his heart.
From vale to vale the' affrighted victims fly,
But catch or give the plague with every sigh;
A touch contaminates the purest veins,
Till the *Black Death* through all the region reigns.*

Comes there no ship again to Greenland's shore?
There comes another: — there shall come no more;
Nor this shall reach an haven: — What are these
Stupendous monuments upon the seas?

* The depopulation of Old Greenland is supposed to have been greatly accelerated by the introduction of the plague, which, under the name of the *Black Death*, made dreadful havoc throughout Europe towards the close of the fourteenth century.

Works of Omnipotence, in wondrous forms,
Immovable as mountains in the storms?
Far as Imagination's eye can roll,
One range of Alpine glaciers to the pole
Flanks the whole eastern coast; and, branching wide,
Arches o'er many a league the' indignant tide,
That works and frets, with unavailing flow,
To mine a passage to the beach below;
Thence from its neck that winter yoke to rend,
And down the gulf the crashing fragments send.
There lies a vessel in this realm of frost,
Not wreck'd, nor stranded, yet for ever lost;
Its keel embedded in the solid mass;
Its glistening sails appear expanded glass;
The transverse ropes with pearls enormous strung,
The yards with icicles grotesquely hung,
Wrapt in the topmost shrouds there rests a boy,
His old sea-faring father's only joy;
Sprung from a race of rovers, ocean-born,
Nursed at the helm, he trod dry land with scorn;
Through fourscore years from port to port he veer'd,
Quicksand, nor rock, nor foe, nor tempest fear'd;
Now cast ashore, though like a hulk he lie,
His son at sea is ever in his eye,
And his prophetic thought, from age to age,
Esteems the waves his offspring's heritage:
He ne'er shall know, in his Norwegian cot,
How brief that son's career, how strange his lot;
Writhed round the mast, and sepulchred in air,
Him shall no worm devour, no vulture tear;

Congeal'd to adamant, his frame shall last,
Though empires change, till time and tide be past.

On deck, in groups embracing as they died,
Singly, erect, or slumbering side by side,
Behold the crew! — They sail'd, with hope elate,
For eastern Greenland: till, ensnared by fate,
In toils that mock'd their utmost strength and skill,
They felt, as by a charm, their ship stand still:
The madness of the wildest gale that blows,
Were mercy to that shudder of repose,
When withering horror struck from heart to heart
The blunt rebound of Death's benumbing dart,
And each, a petrifaction at his post,
Look'd on yon father, and gave up the ghost; *
He meekly kneeling, with his hands upraised,
His beard of driven snow, eyes fix'd and glazed,
Alone among the dead shall yet survive,
— The' imperishable dead, that seem alive;
— The' immortal dead, whose spirits, breaking free,
Bore his last words into eternity,
While with a seraph's zeal, a Christian's love,
Till his tongue fail'd, he spoke of joys above.

* The Danish Chronicle says, that the Greenland colonists were tributary to the kings of Norway from the year 1023; soon after which they embraced Christianity. In its more flourishing period this province is stated to have been divided into a hundred parishes, under the superintendence of a bishop. From 1120 to 1408 the succession of seventeen bishops is recorded. In the last-mentioned year, Andrew, ordained bishop of Greenland by Askill, archbishop of Drontheim, sailed for his diocese, but whether he arrived there, or was cast away, was never known. To his imagined fate this episode alludes.

Now motionless, amidst the icy air,
He breathes from marble lips unutter'd prayer.
The clouds condensed, with dark, unbroken hue
Of stormy purple, overhang his view,
Save in the west, to which he strains his sight,
One golden streak, that grows intensely bright,
Till thence the' emerging sun, with lightning blaze,
Pours the whole quiver of his arrowy rays;
The smitten rocks to instant diamond turn,
And round the' expiring saint such visions burn,
As if the gates of Paradise were thrown
Wide open to receive his soul; — 't is flown.
The glory vanishes, and over all
Cimmerian darkness spreads her funeral pall.

Morn shall return, and noon, and eve, and night
Meet here with interchanging shade and light;
But from this bark no timber shall decay,
Of these cold forms no feature pass away;
Perennial ice around the' encrusted bow,
The peopled deck, and full-rigg'd masts shall grow,
Till from the sun himself the whole be hid,
Or spied beneath a crystal pyramid;
As in pure amber, with divergent lines,
A rugged shell emboss'd with sea-weed shines.
From age to age increased with annual snow,
This new *Mont Blanc* among the clouds may glow,
Whose conic peak, that earliest greets the dawn,
And latest from the sun's shut eye withdrawn,
Shall from the zenith, through incumbent gloom,
Burn like a lamp upon this naval tomb.

But when the' archangel's trumpet sounds on high,
The pile shall burst to atoms through the sky,
And leave its dead, upstarting at the call,
Naked and pale, before the Judge of all.

Once more to Greenland's long forsaken beach,
Which foot of man again shall never reach,
Imagination wings her flight, explores
The march of Pestilence along the shores,
And sees how Famine in his steps hath paced,
While Winter laid the soil for ever waste.
Dwellings are heaps of fall'n or falling stones,
The charnel-houses of unburied bones,
On which obscene and prowling monsters fed,
But with the ravin in their jaws fell dead.
Thus while Destruction, blasting youth and age,
Raged till it wanted victims for its rage;
Love, the last feeling that from life retires,
Blew the faint spark of his unfuell'd fires.
In the cold sunshine of yon narrow dell
Affection lingers; — *there* two lovers dwell,
Greenland's whole family; nor long forlorn,
There comes a visitant; a babe is born.
O'er his meek helplessness the parents smiled;
'T was Hope; — for Hope is every mother's child:
Then seem'd they, in that world of solitude,
The Eve and Adam of a race renew'd.
Brief happiness! too perilous to last;
The moon hath wax'd and wan'd, and all is past:
Behold the end: — one morn, athwart the wall,
They mark'd the shadow of a reindeer fall,

Bounding in tameless freedom o'er the snow;
The father track'd him, and with fatal bow
Smote down the victim; but before his eyes,
A rabid she-bear pounced upon the prize;
A shaft into the spoiler's flank he sent,
She turn'd in wrath, and limb from limb had rent
The hunter; but his dagger's plunging steel,
With riven bosom, made the monster reel;
Unvanquish'd, both to closer combat flew,
Assailants each, till each the other slew;
Mingling their blood from mutual wounds, they lay
Stretch'd on the carcass of their antler'd prey.

Meanwhile his partner waits, her heart at rest,
No burden but her infant on her breast:
With him she slumbers, or with him she plays,
And tells him all her dreams of future days,
Asks him a thousand questions, feigns replies,
And reads whate'er she wishes in his eyes.
— Red evening comes; no husband's shadow falls,
Where fell the reindeer's o'er the latticed walls:
'T is night; no footstep sounds towards her door;
The day returns, — but he returns no more.
In frenzy forth she sallies; and with cries,
To which no voice except her own replies
In frightful echoes, starting all around,
Where human voice again shall never sound,
She seeks him, finds him not; some angel-guide
In mercy turns her from the corpse aside;
Perhaps his own freed spirit, lingering near,
Who waits to waft her to a happier sphere,

But leads her first, at evening, to their cot,
Where lies the little one, all day forgot;
Imparadised in sleep she finds him there,
Kisses his cheek, and breathes a mother's prayer.
Three days she languishes, nor can she shed
One tear, between the living and the dead;
When her lost spouse comes o'er the widow's thought,
The pangs of memory are to madness wrought;
But when her suckling's eager lips are felt,
Her heart would fain — but oh! it cannot — melt;
At length it breaks, while on her lap he lies,
With baby wonder gazing in her eyes.
Poor orphan! mine is not a hand to trace
Thy little story, last of all thy race!
Not long thy sufferings; cold and colder grown,
The arms that clasp thee chill thy limbs to stone.
— 'T is done: — from Greenland's coast, the latest sigh
Bore infant innocence beyond the sky.

END OF CANTO V.

APPENDIX TO GREENLAND.

CANTO I.

(A), page 9.

THE story of the introduction of Christianity among the Sclavonic tribes is interesting. The Bulgarians, being borderers on the Greek empire, frequently made predatory incursions on the Imperial territory. On one occasion the sister of Bogaris, King of the Bulgarians, was taken prisoner, and carried to Constantinople. Being a royal captive, she was treated with great honor, and diligently instructed in the doctrines of the Gospel, of the truth of which she became so deeply convinced, that she desired to be baptized; and when, in 845, the Emperor Michael III. made peace with the Bulgarians, she returned to her country a pious and zealous Christian. Being earnestly concerned for the conversion of her brother and his people, she wrote to Constantinople for teachers to instruct them in the way of righteousness. Two distinguished bishops of the Greek Church, Cyrillus and Methodius, were accordingly sent into Bulgaria. The King Bogaris, who heretofore had resisted conviction, conceived a particular affection for Methodius, who, being a skilful painter, was desired by him, in the spirit of a barbarian, to compose a picture exhibiting the most horrible devices. Methodius took a happy advantage of this strange request, and painted the day of judgment in a style so terrific, and explained its scenes to his royal master in language so awful and affecting, that Bogaris was awakened, made a profession of the true faith, and was baptized by the name of Michael, in honor of his benefactor the Greek Emperor. His subjects, according to the fashion of the times, some by choice, and others from constraint, adopted their master's religion. To Cyrillus is attributed the translation of the Scriptures still in use among the descendants of the Sclavonian tribes, which adhere to the Greek Church; and this is probably the most ancient European version of the Bible in a living tongue.

But notwithstanding this triumphant introduction of Christianity among these fierce nations (including the Bohemians and Moravians), multitudes adhered to idolatry, and among the nobles especially many continued Pagans, and in open or secret enmity against the new religion and its professors. In Bohemia, Duke Borziwog, having embraced the Gospel, was expelled by his chieftains, and one Stoymirus, who had been thirteen years in exile, and who was believed to be a heathen, was chosen by them as their prince. He being, however, soon detected in Christian worship, was deposed, and Borziwog recalled. The latter died soon after his restoration, leaving his widow, Ludomilla, regent during the minority of her son Wratislaus, who married a noble lady, named Drahomira. The young duchess, to ingratiate herself with her husband and her mother-in-law, affected to embrace Christianity, while in her heart she remained an implacable enemy to it. Her husband dying early, left her with two infant boys. Wenceslaus, the elder, was taken by his grandmother, the pious Ludomilla, and carefully educated in Christian principles; the younger, Boleslas, was not less carefully educated in hostility against them by Drahomira; who, seizing the government during the minority of her children, shut up the churches, forbade the clergy either to preach or teach in schools, and imprisoned, banished, or put to death those who disobeyed her edicts against the Gospel. But when her eldest son, Wenceslaus, became of age, he was persuaded by his grandmother and the principal Christian nobles to take possession of the government, which was his inheritance. He did so, and began his reign by removing his pagan mother and brother to a distance from the metropolis. Drahomira, transported with rage, resolved to rid herself of her mother-in-law, whose influence over Wenceslaus was predominant. She found two heathen assassins ready for her purpose, who, stealing unperceived into Ludomilla's oratory, fell upon her as she entered it for evening prayers, threw a rope round her neck, and strangled her. The remorseless Drahomira next plotted against Wenceslaus, to deprive him of the government; but her intrigues miscarrying, she proposed to her heathen son to murder him. An opportunity soon offered. On the birth of a son, Boleslas invited his Christian brother to visit him, and be present at a pretended ceremony of blessing the infant. Wenceslaus attended, and was treated with unwonted kindness; but, suspecting treachery, he could not sleep in his brother's house. He therefore went to spend the night in the church. Here, as he lay defenceless in an imagined sanctuary, Boleslas, instigated by their unnatural mother, surprised and slew him with his sabre. The murderer immediately usurped the sovereignty, and commenced a cruel persecution against the Christians. which was terminated by the interference of the Roman Emperor Otto I., who made war upon Boleslas, reduced him to the condition of a vassal, and gave peace to his persecuted subjects. This happened in the year 943.

(B), page 11.

The genuine followers of John Huss never approved of the war for religion carried on by Ziska, though many of them were identically involved in it. Rokyzan, a Calixtine, having with his party made a compromise with their sovereign and the priests, by which they were allowed the use of the cup in the sacrament, was made archbishop of Prague in the year 1435; and thenceforward, though he had been fully convinced of the truth of the doctrines promulgated by Huss, he became a treacherous friend or an open enemy of his followers, as it happened to serve the purposes of his ambition. The Pope, however, refused to confirm him in his new dignity, unless he would relinquish the cup; on which, for a time, he made great pretensions of undertaking a thorough reform in the church. All who hoped any thing good of him were disappointed, and none more than his pious nephew Gregorius, who in vain, on behalf of the peace-loving Hussites, besought him to proceed in the work of church-regeneration. He refused peremptorily, at length, after having greatly dissimulated and temporized. His refusal was the immediate cause of the commencement of the Church of the United Brethren, in that form in which it has been recognized for nearly four hundred years. They were no sooner known, however, as "*Fratres legis Christi*," Brethren according to the rule of Christ, than they were persecuted as heretics. Among others, Gregorius, who is styled the "Patriarch of the Brethren," was apprehended at a private meeting with a number of his people. The judge who executed the royal authority, on entering the room, used these remarkable words:—"It is written, all that will live godly in Christ Jesus shall suffer persecution; therefore, follow me, by command of the higher powers." They followed, and were sentenced to the torture. On the rack, Gregorius fell into a swoon, and all present supposed him to be dead. Hereupon his apostate uncle Rokyzan hastened to the spot, and falling upon his neck, with tears and loud lamentations bewailed him, exclaiming,—O, my dear Gregorius! would God I were where thou art!" His nephew, however, revived, and was set at liberty. He afterwards, according to tradition, declared that in his trance he had seen a vision;—a tree, covered with leaves and blossoms and fruits, on which many beautiful birds were feeding and melodiously singing. Under it was a shepherd's boy, and near at hand three venerable old men (as guardians of the tree), whose habiliments and countenances were those of the three persons who, several years afterwards, were consecrated the first bishops of the Church of the United Brethren, by Stephen, the last bishop of the Waldenses.

(C), page 12.

Comenius afterwards visited and resided in various parts of Germany, Holland, and England; everywhere, on his travels, recommending, with earnestness and importunity, the case of his oppressed brethren in Bohemia and Moravia to men in power. But his appeals were in vain; and when, at the peace of Westphalia, in 1648, he found that nothing was provided for their protection in the free exercise of their religion, he published an affecting representation of the peculiar hardships of their church, in which he observed: — "We justly, indeed, deserve to bear the wrath of Almighty God; but will such men (alluding to the Protestant diplomatists and their constituent authorities) be able to justify their actions before God, who, forgetting the common cause of all Protestants, and the old covenants amongst us, neglect to assist those who are oppressed in the same engagements? Having made peace for themselves, they never gave it a thought, that the Bohemians and Moravians, who *at the first, and for so many centuries*, asserted the truth in opposition to Popery, were likewise worthy to be mutually considered by them; that the light of the Gospel, which first was enkindled and put upon the candlestick in the Brethren's church, might not now be extinguished, as it appears to be. This afflicted people, therefore, which on account of its faithful adherence to the apostolic doctrines, following the footsteps of the primitive church, and the instructions of the holy fathers, has been so much hated, persecuted, tossed to and fro, and even forsaken by those of its own household, and now finds mercy from no man; — this afflicted people has nothing left, but to cast itself upon the aid of the eternally merciful Lord God, and with the ancient prophet, when his nation was overthrown by its enemies, to exclaim, — 'For these things I weep; mine eye, mine eye runneth down with water, because the Comforter that should relieve my soul is far from me.' Lam. i. 16. — But Thou, O Lord God! who abidest for ever and ever, and whose throne is eternal, why wilt Thou forget us, and even forsake us in this extremity? O bring us, Lord, again to Thyself, that we may return to our homes. Renew our days as of old." In 1649, Comenius published a history of the Brethren's Church, which he dedicated, as his "last will and testament," to *the Church of England*, to preserve for the successors of the brethren in future ages, as to the last hour of his life he cherished the hope of their revival and establishment in peace and freedom. — This work was translated from the original Latin, and published in London in 1661.

(D), page 13.

Previous to the Reformation, for about fifty years, the prisons in Bohemia, and especially at Prague, were filled, from time to time, in consequence of special decrees, with members of the Brethren's Church. Michael, one of their first bishops, was long under rigorous confinement. Many perished in deep dungeons, with cold and hunger; others were cruelly tortured. The remainder were obliged to seek refuge in thick forests, and to hide themselves by day in caverns and recesses among the rocks. Fearing to be betrayed in the daytime by the smoke, they kindled their fires only at night, around which they employed their time in reading the Scriptures, and in prayer. If they were under the necessity of going out in the snow, either to seek provisions or to visit their neighbors, they always walked behind one another, each in his turn treading in the footsteps of the first, and the last dragging a piece of brushwood after him, to obliterate the track, or to make it appear as if some poor peasant had been to the woods to fetch a bundle of sticks. With the first Reformers, Luther, Calvin, Zuinglius, Melancthon, Bucer, and Capito, the Brethren held the most friendly correspondence, and by all were acknowledged to be a true apostolical church. The strictness of their church-discipline, however, and the difference which subsisted among these great men themselves on that general subject, as well as the insulated locality of the Brethren, probably were the causes why they remained still totally distinct from any of the new Christian societies which were then instituted. *After* the Reformation, especially about the beginning and till the middle of the seventeenth century, they were exposed to the same kind of persecutions and proscriptions which their ancestors had suffered. After the death of the Emperor Rudolph, in 1612, the resolutions of the Council of Trent were decreed to be put in force against all Protestants in Bohemia. This occasioned a civil war, like that of the Hussites. The Brethren, though they are understood to have taken very little share in this defence of the truth, by weapons of carnal warfare, were nevertheless exposed to all the vindictive cruelty by which the Protestants in Bohemia were nearly extirpated, after their defeat by the Imperialists, on the White Mountain, near Prague, in 1620. On the 21st June, 1621, no less than *twenty-seven* of the Patrons (*Defensores*) of the Protestant cause, principally nobles and men of distinction, were beheaded, who all died as faithful witnesses and martyrs to the religion of Christ. This execution was followed by a decree of banishment against all ministers of the Brethren's churches in Bohemia and Moravia. Many hundred families, both noble and plebeian, fled into the neighboring provinces. Emigration, however, was rendered as difficult as possible to the common people, who were strictly watched by the emissaries of persecution. Many thousands, notwithstanding, gradually made their escape, and joined their ministers in exile; others, who from age, infirmity, or the burden of large families, could not do the same, remained in their country, but were compelled to worship God, after the manner of their forefathers, in secret only; for thenceforward neither churches nor schools for Protestants were allowed to exist in Bohemia and Moravia. Search was made for their Bibles and religious books, which were burnt in piles, and in some places under the gallows.

(E), page 15.

After the lapse of nearly a century, during which the refugees of the Brethren's churches, in Saxony, Poland, and Prussia were nearly lost among the people with whom they associated, and the small remnant that continued in Moravia kept up the fire on their family altars, while in their churches it was utterly extinct, a new persecution against this small remnant drove many of them from their homes, who, under the conduct of Christian David, finding an asylum on the estates of Count Zinzendorf, founded near Bertholsdorf the first congregation of the revived church of the United Brethren. On the 8th of June, 1722, Christian David, with four of the first fugitives that arrived in Lusatia, were presented to Count Zinzendorf's grandmother, who instantly gave them protection, and promised to furnish them with the means of establishing themselves on one of her family estates. Count Zinzendorf himself gives the following account of the circumstances under which he fixed upon the situation for these settlers. He proposed a district called the Hutberg, near the high road to Zittau. It was objected, by some who knew the place, that there was no water there: he answered, "God is able to help!" and the following morning early he repaired thither to observe the rising of the vapors, that he might determine where a well might be dug. The next morning he again visited the place alone, and satisfied himself of its eligibility for a settlement. He adds, "I laid the misery and desire of these people before God with many tears; beseeching Him that his hand might be with me and frustrate my measures, if they were in any way displeasing to Him. I said further to the Lord, — 'Upon this spot I will, in thy name, build the first house for them.' In the mean time the Moravians returned to the farm-house (where they had been previously lodged), having brought their families thither out of their native country. These I assisted to the best of my power, and then went to Hennersdorf to acquaint my lady (his grandmother aforementioned) with the resolution I had taken. She made no objection, and immediately sent the poor strangers a cow, that they might be furnished with milk for their little children; and she ordered me to show them the trees to be cut down for their building."

CANTO III.

(F), page 35.

Crantz says, — "On the 10th of April the Brethren went on board the king's ship Caritas, Captain Hildebrande, accompanied with many sincere wishes for blessing from the court (of Denmark) and all benevolent minds. The congregation at Herrnhut had a custom, from the year 1729, before the commencement of a year, to compile a little manual, containing a text of Holy Scripture for every day in the same, and each illustrated or applied by a verse annexed, out of the hymn-book. This text was called the word of the day; it was given to be the subject of meditation with each member of the church in private, and of discourse by the ministers in the public meeting. Many a time it has been found that the word of the day, on which some peculiar event occurred, has remarkably coincided with it. Thus on this 10th of April, when our brethren set sail (from Copenhagen) on a mission, which often afterwards seemed to baffle all hope, the word was (Heb. xi. 1), 'Faith is the substance of things hoped for, the evidence of things not seen.'

'We view Him, whom no eye can see,
With faith's perspective steadfastly.'

In this confidence they set sail, nor did they suffer themselves to be confounded by any of the unspeakable difficulties of the following years, till they and we at last beheld the completion of what they hoped for by faith. They had a speedy, and, excepting some storms, a commodious voyage. They sailed by Shetland, April 22d, passing there out of the North into the West Sea, or long reach, and entered Davis's Straits about the beginning of May. On the 6th they fell among some floating ice, in a thick fog, and the next day were assailed by a terrible tempest; but this very tempest drove the ice so far asunder, that it also dissipated their fears. The 13th they descried land; but on the same day, after a total eclipse of the sun, there arose a violent storm, that lasted four days and nights, and drove them sixty leagues back. May the 20th, they entered Ball's River, after a voyage of six weeks. The word of the day was, 'The peace of God, which passeth all understanding, keep your hearts and minds through Jesus Christ.' By this they were frequently encouraged in the first years ensuing, amidst all the opposition which they encountered, and the small prospect of the conversion of the heathens."

(G), page 43.

The Greenlanders believe that the sun and moon are sister and brother. They, with other children, were once playing together in the dark, when Aninga behaving rudely to his sister Malina, she rubbed her hands in the soot about the extinguished lamp and smeared his face, that she might discover by daylight who was her tormentor; and thus the dusky spots on the moon had their origin; for she, struggling to escape, slipped out of his arms, soared aloft, and became the sun. He followed up into the firmament, and was transformed into the moon; but as he has never been able to rise so high as she, he continues running after her, with the vain hope of overtaking her. When he is tired and hungry, in his last quarter, he sets out from his house a seal-hunting, on a sledge drawn by four great dogs, and stays several days abroad to recruit and fatten; and this produces the full moon. He rejoices when the women die, and Malina, in revenge, rejoices when the men die; therefore the men keep at home during an eclipse of the sun, and the women during an eclipse of the moon. When he is in eclipse, Aninga prowls about the dwellings of the Greenlanders, to plague the females, and steal provisions and skins, nay even to kill those persons who have not duly observed the laws of temperance. At these times they hide their most precious goods; and the men carry kettles and chests to the tops of their houses, and rattle upon them with cudgels to frighten away the moon, and make him return to his place in the sky. During an eclipse of the sun, the men skulk in terror into the darkest corners, while the women pinch the ears of their dogs; and if these cry out, it is a sure omen that the end of the world is not yet come: for as dogs existed before men, according to Greenland logic, they must have a quicker foresight into futurity. Should the dogs be mute, (which of course they never are, under such ill treatment,) then the dissolution of all things must be at hand. — See Crantz

CANTO IV.

(H), page 56.

An Icelander, named Bioern, in the year 1001, following his father, who had emigrated to Greenland, is said to have been driven by a storm to the south-west, where he discovered a fine champaign country coverėd with forests. He did not tarry long there, but made the best of his way back again, north-east, for Greenland, which he reached in safety. The tidings of his adventure being rumored abroad there, one Leif, the son of Eric the Red, a famous navigator, being ambitious of acquiring fame, by discovering and planting new lands, fitted out a vessel, with thirty-five men, and sailed with Bioern on board, in search of the south-west country. They arrived, in due time, at a low woody coast, and sailed up a river to a spacious lake, which communicated by it with the sea. The soil was exceedingly fruitful, the wāters abounded with fish, particularly salmon, and the climate was mild. Leif and his party wintered there, and observed that, on the shortest day, the sun rose about eight o'clock, which may correspond with the forty-ninth degree of latitude, and denotes the situation of Newfoundland, or the river St. Lawrence in Canada. When they built their huts, after landing, they one day missed a German mariner named Tyrker, whom, after a long search, they found in the woods, dancing with delight. On being asked what made him so merry, he answered, that he had been eating such grapes as those of which wine was made in his native country. When Leif saw and tasted the fruit himself, he called the new region Vünland, or Wineland. Crantz, who gives this account, on various authorities, adds in a note, that " well-flavored wild grapes are known to grow in the forests of Canada, but no good wine has been produced from them." — After the return of Leif to Greenland, many voyages were undertaken to Wineland, and some colonies established there. One Thorfin, an Icelander, who had married a Greenland heiress, Gudrid, the widow of the third son of Eric the Red, by whom he obtained the inheritance of Wineland, ventured thither with sixty-five men and five women; taking cattle and implements of husbandry with them, for the purpose of building and planting. The natives (probably the Esquimaux) found them thus settled, and were glad to barter with their furs and skins in exchange for iron instruments, etc. One of these barbarians, however, having stolen an axe, was dolt enough to try its edge on his companion's skull, which cost the poor wretch his life; whereupon a third, wiser than either, threw the murderous weapon into the sea. — Commerce with Wineland is reported to have been carried on for upwards of an hundred years afterwards.

(I), page 61.

The ancestors of the modern inhabitants first appeared on the western coast of Greenland in the fourteenth century, and are generally supposed to have overpowered the few Norwegians scattered in that quarter. They are called Skraellings, a word of uncertain etymology, but most probably a corruption of Karallit, or people, by which they designated themselves. Of their origin nothing can be ascertained. It seems, on the whole, not incredible (from evidence and arguments which need not be quoted here), that they are the descendants of Tartarean rovers, gradually emigrating from the heart of Asia, crossing over into West America, traversing the northern latitudes of that continent, and settling or wandering, as suited their convenience, till the foremost hordes reached Canada and Labrador; from whence the first Skraellings may have found a passage, by land or sea, to Greenland. That the Greenlanders are of the same stock with the Esquimaux, is obvious from the remarkable correspondence between their persons, dress, habitations, boats, and implements of hunting and fishing, as well as the similarity of manners, customs, superstitions, and language. Of these more may be said hereafter, should the poem of GREENLAND ever be completed. Meanwhile the slight sketch given in the context may suffice. The following description of a Greenlander's fishing-boat, or kayak, will, however, be useful to illustrate the passage. The kayak is six yards in length, pointed at the head and stern and shaped like a weaver's shuttle; it is at the same time scarcely a foot and a half broad over the middle, and not more than a foot deep. It is built of a slender skeleton of wood, consisting of a keel, and long side-laths, with cross-ribs, like hoops but not quite round. The whole is covered with seal's skin. In the middle of this covering there is a round aperture, supported with a strong rim of wood or bone. The Greenlander slips into the cavity with his feet, and sits down upon a board covered with soft skins; he then tucks his water-pelt or great coat, so tight about him (the rim of the opening forming a girdle round his loins), that no water can penetrate into his little skiff. His lance, harpoon, and fishing tackle are all arranged in due order before him. His pautik, or oar, (made of red deal, and strengthened with bone inlaid,) he uses with admirable dexterity. This, except when he is using his weapon, he grasps with both hands in the middle, striking the water on either side alternately, by which means he can sail at the rate of twenty or even twenty-four leagues a day. In his kayak the Greenlander fears no storm, so long as he can keep his oar, which enables him to sit upright among the roughest breakers, or if overturned, while the head is downward under water, with one stroke he can recover himself; but if he loses his oar, in a high sea, he loses all. No European has ever yet been able to learn to manage a kayak except in calm weather, and when he had nothing to do but to row; to fish in it has been found impracticable to any but the natives themselves, trained from their infancy to all the hardy exercises which constituted, before the introduction of Christianity, the whole education of the poor barbarians.

MISCELLANEOUS POEMS.

MISCELLANEOUS POEMS.

HOPE.

IMITATED FROM THE ITALIAN OF SERAFINO AQUILANO.

Hope, unyielding to despair,
Springs for ever fresh and fair;
Earth's serenest prospects fly,
Hope's enchantments never die.

At Fortune's frown, in evil hour,
Though honor, wealth, and friends depart,
She cannot drive, with all her power,
This lonely solace from the heart:
And while this the soul sustains,
Fortune still unchanged remains;
Wheresoe'er her wheel she guides,
Hope upon the circle rides.

The Syrens, deep in ocean's caves,
Sing while abroad the tempests roar,
Expecting soon the frantic waves
To ripple on a smiling shore:

In the whirlwind, o'er the spray,
They behold the halcyon play;
And through midnight clouds afar
Hope lights up the morning star.

This pledge of bliss in future years
Makes smooth and easy every toil;
The swain, who sows the waste with tears,
In fancy reaps a teeming soil:
What though mildew blight his joy,
Frost or flood his crops destroy,
War compel his feet to roam,
Hope still carols Harvest Home!

The monarch exiled from his realm,
The slave in fetters at the oar,
The seaman sinking by the helm,
The captive on his dungeon floor;
All through peril, pain, and death,
Fondly cling to parting breath;
Glory, freedom, power, are past,
But the dream of Hope will last.

Weary and faint, with sickness worn,
Blind, lame, and deaf, and bent with age,
By man the load of life is borne
To his last step of pilgrimage:
Though the branch no longer shoot,
Vigor lingers at the root,
And in Winter's dreariest day
Hope foretells returning May.

When, wrung with guilt, the wretch would end
His gloomy days in sudden night,
Hope comes, an unexpected friend,
To win him back to hated light:
    " Hold!" she cries; and from his hand
    Plucks the suicidal brand;
    " Now await a happier doom,
    Hope will cheer thee to the tomb."

When virtue droops, as comforts fail,
And sore afflictions press the mind,
Sweet Hope prolongs her pleasing tale,
Till all the world again looks kind:
    Round the good man's dying bed,
    Were the wreck of Nature spread,
    Hope would set his spirit free,
    Crying — " Immortality!"

A MOTHER'S LOVE.

A Mother's Love, — how sweet the name!
  What *is* a Mother's love?
— A noble, pure, and tender flame,
  Enkindled from above,
To bless a heart of earthly mould;
The warmest love that *can* grow cold;
  This is a Mother's Love.

To bring a helpless babe to light,
  Then, while it lies forlorn,
To gaze upon that dearest sight,
  And feel herself new-born,
In its existence lose her own,
And live and breathe in it alone;
  This is a Mother's Love.

Its weakness in her arms to bear;
  To cherish on her breast,
Feed it from Love's own fountain there,
  And lull it there to rest;
Then, while it slumbers, watch its breath,
As if to guard from instant death;
  This is a Mother's Love.

To mark its growth from day to day,
  Its opening charms admire,
Catch from its eye the earliest ray
  Of intellectual fire;
To smile and listen while it talks,
And lend a finger when it walks;
  This is a Mother's Love.

And can a Mother's Love grow cold?
  Can she forget her boy?
His pleading innocence behold,
  Nor weep for grief — for joy?
A Mother may forget her child,
While wolves devour it on the wild;
  Is *this* a Mother's Love?

Ten thousand voices answer "No!"
  Ye clasp your babes and kiss;
Your bosoms yearn, your eyes o'erflow;
  Yet, ah! remember this, —
The infant, rear'd alone for earth,
May live, may die, — to curse his birth;
  — Is *this* a Mother's Love?

A parent's heart may prove a snare;
  The child she loves so well,
Her hand may lead, with gentlest care,
  Down the smooth road to hell;
Nourish its frame, — destroy its mind:
Thus do the blind mislead the blind,
  Even with a Mother's Love.

Blest infant! whom his mother taught
  Early to seek the Lord,
And pour'd upon his dawning thought
  The dayspring of the word;
This was the lesson to her son
— Time is Eternity begun:
  Behold that Mother's Love.*

Blest Mother! who, in wisdom's path
  By her own parent trod,
Thus taught her son to flee the wrath,
  And know the fear, of God:
Ah, youth! like him enjoy your prime;
Begin Eternity in time,
  Taught by that Mother's Love.

That Mother's Love! — how sweet the name!
  What *was* that Mother's Love?
— The noblest, purest, tenderest flame,
  That kindles from above,
Within a heart of earthly mould,
As much of heaven as heart can hold,
Nor through eternity grows cold:
  This was that Mother's Love.

* 2 Tim. i. 5, and iii. 14, 15.

1814.

THE TIME-PIECE.

Who is *He* so swiftly flying,
His career no eye can see?
Who are *They*, so early dying,
From their birth they cease to be?
Time: — behold his pictured face!
Moments: — can you count their race?

Though, with aspect deep-dissembling,
Here he feigns unconscious sleep,
Round and round this circle trembling,
Day and night his symbols creep,
While unseen, through earth and sky
His unwearying pinions ply.

Hark! what petty pulses, beating,
Spring new moments into light;
Every pulse, its stroke repeating,
Sends its moment back to night;
Yet not one of all the train
Comes uncall'd, or flits in vain.

In the highest realms of glory,
Spirits trace, before the throne,
On eternal scrolls, the story
Of each little moment flown;

Every deed, and word, and thought,
Through the whole creation wrought.

Were the volume of a minute
Thus to mortal sight unroll'd,
More of sin and sorrow in it,
More of man, might we behold,
Than on History's broadest page
In the relics of an age.

Who could bear the revelation?
Who abide the sudden test?
— With instinctive consternation,
Hands would cover every breast,
Loudest tongues at once be hush'd,
Pride in all its writhings crush'd.

Who, with leer malign exploring,
On his neighbor's shame durst look?
Would not each, intensely poring
On that record in the book,
Which his inmost soul reveal'd,
Wish its leaves for ever seal'd?

Seal'd they are for years, and ages,
Till, — the earth's last circuit run,
Empire changed through all its stages,
Risen and set the latest sun, —
On the sea and on the land,
Shall a midnight Angel stand: —

Stand ; — and, while the' abysses tremble,
Swear that Time shall be no more :
Quick and Dead shall then assemble,
Men and Demons range before
That tremendous judgment-seat,
Where both worlds at issue meet.

Time himself, with all his legions,
Days, *Months*, *Years*, since Nature's birth,
Shall revive, — and from all regions,
Singling out the sons of earth,
With their glory or disgrace,
Charge their spenders face to face.

Every moment of my being
Then shall pass before mine eyes :
— God, all-searching ! God, all-seeing !
Oh ! appease them, ere they rise :
Warn'd I fly, I fly to Thee ;
God, be merciful to me !

Liverpool, 1816.

STANZAS

TO THE MEMORY OF THE REV. THOMAS SPENCER, OF LIVERPOOL,

WHO WAS DROWNED, WHILE BATHING IN THE TIDE, ON THE 5TH OF AUGUST, 1811, IN HIS 21ST YEAR.

"Thy way is in the sea, and thy path in the great waters; and thy footsteps are not known." — *Psalm* lxxvii. 19.

I WILL not sing a mortal's praise;
To Thee I consecrate my lays,
To whom my powers belong!
These gifts upon thine altar strown
O GOD! accept — accept thine own;
My gifts are Thine, — be Thine alone
The glory of my song.

In earth and ocean, sky and air,
All that is excellent and fair,
Seen, felt, or understood,
From one eternal cause descends,
To one eternal centre tends,
With GOD begins, continues, ends,
The source and stream of good.

I worship not the Sun at noon,
The wandering Stars, the changing Moon,

The Wind, the Flood, the Flame;
I will not bow the votive knee
To Wisdom, Virtue, Liberty;
"There *is* no God but God" for me;
— Jehovah is his name.

Him through all nature I explore,
Him in his creatures I adore,
Around, beneath, above;
But clearest in the human mind,
His bright resemblance when I find,
Grandeur with purity combined,
I most admire and love.

Oh! there was One, — on earth awhile
He dwelt; — but transient as a smile
That turns into a tear,
His beauteous image pass'd us by;
He came, like lightning from the sky,
He seem'd as dazzling to the eye,
As prompt to disappear.

Mild in his undissembling mien,
Were genius, candor, meekness seen;
— The lips, that loved the truth;
The single eye, whose glance sublime
Look'd to eternity through time;
The soul, whose hopes were wont to climb
Above the joys of youth.

Of old, before the lamp grew dark,
Reposing near the curtain'd ark,
The child of Hannah's prayer
Heard, through the temple's silent round,
A living voice, nor knew the sound,
— That thrice alarm'd him, ere he found
The Lord, who chose him there.*

Thus early call'd, and strongly moved,
A prophet from a child, approved,
SPENCER his course began;
From strength to strength, from grace to grace,
Swiftest and foremost in the race,
He carried victory in his face;
He triumph'd as he ran.

How short his day! — the glorious prize,
To our slow hearts and failing eyes,
Appear'd too quickly won:
— The warrior rush'd into the field,
With arm invincible to wield
The Spirit's sword, the Spirit's shield,
When, lo! the fight was done.

The loveliest star of evening's train
Sets early in the western main,
And leaves the world in night;
The brightest star of morning's host,
Scarce risen, in brighter beams is lost;

* 1 Sam. iii.

Thus sunk his form on ocean's coast,
  Thus sprang his soul to light.

Who shall forbid the eye to weep,
That saw him, from the ravening deep,
  Pluck'd like the lion's prey?
For ever bowed his honor'd head,
The spirit in a moment fled,
The heart of friendship cold and dead,
  The limbs a wreath of clay!

Revolving his mysterious lot,
I mourn him, but I praise him not;
  Glory to God be given,
Who sent him, like the radiant bow,
His covenant of peace to show;
Athwart the breaking storm to glow,
  Then vanish into heaven.

O Church! to whom that youth was dear,
The Angel of thy mercies here,
  Behold the path he trod,
"A milky way" through midnight skies!
— Behold the grave in which he lies;
Even from this dust thy prophet cries,
  "*Prepare to meet thy GOD.*"

HUMAN LIFE.

JOB XIV.

How few and evil are thy days,
Man, of a woman born!
Trouble and peril haunt thy ways:
— Forth like a flower at morn,
The tender infant springs to light,
Youth blossoms with the breeze,
Age, withering age, is cropt ere night,
— Man like a shadow flees.

And dost Thou look on such an one?
Will God to judgment call
A worm, for what a worm hath done
Against the Lord of all?
As fail the waters from the deep,
As summer brooks run dry,
Man lieth down in dreamless sleep:
— Our life is vanity.

Man lieth down, no more to wake,
Till yonder arching sphere
Shall with a roll of thunder break,
And nature disappear.
— Oh! hide me, till thy wrath be past,
Thou, who canst kill or save;
Hide me, where hope may anchor fast
In my Redeemer's grave.

THE VISIBLE CREATION.

THE GOD of Nature and of Grace
In all his works appears;
His goodness through the earth we trace,
His grandeur in the spheres.

Behold this fair and fertile globe,
By Him in wisdom plann'd;
'T was He who girded, like a robe,
The ocean round the land.

Lift to the firmament your eye,
Thither his path pursue;
His glory, boundless as the sky,
O'erwhelms the wondering view.

He bows the heavens — the mountains stand
A highway for their God;
He walks amidst the desert land,
— 'T is Eden where He trod.

The forests in his strength rejoice;
Hark! on the evening breeze,
As once of old, the LORD GOD's voice
Is heard among the trees.

Here on the hills He feeds his herds,
His flocks on yonder plains:
His praise is warbled by the birds;
— O could we catch their strains!

— Mount with the lark, and bear our song
Up to the gates of light,
Or with the nightingale prolong
Our numbers through the night!

In every stream his bounty flows,
Diffusing joy and wealth;
In every breeze his spirit blows,
— The breath of life and health.

His blessings fall in plenteous showers
Upon the lap of earth,
That teems with foliage, fruit, and flowers,
And rings with infant mirth.

If God hath made this world so fair,
Where sin and death abound,
How beautiful beyond compare
Will Paradise be found!

SONNET.

IMITATED FROM THE ITALIAN OF GAETANA PASSERINI.

If in the field I meet a smiling flower,
Methinks it whispers, " God created me,
And I to Him devote my little hour,
In lonely sweetness and humility."
If, where the forest's darkest shadows lower,
A serpent quick and venomous I see,
It seems to say, — " I, too, extol the power
Of Him, who caused me, at his will, to be."

The fountain purling, and the river strong,
The rocks, the trees, the mountains raise one song;
" Glory to God ! " re-echoes in mine ear :
Faithless were I, in wilful error blind,
Did I not Him in all his creatures find,
His voice through heaven, and earth, and ocean hear.

SONNET.

IMITATED FROM THE ITALIAN OF GIAMBATTISTA COTTA.

I SAW the' eternal GOD, in robes of light,
Rise from his throne, — to judgment forth he came ;
His presence pass'd before me, like the flame
That fires the forest in the depth of night :
Whirlwind and storm, amazement and affright,
Compass'd his path, and shook all Nature's frame,
When from the heaven of heavens, with loud acclaim,
To earth he wing'd his instantaneous flight.

As some triumphal oak, whose boughs have spread
Their changing foliage through a thousand years,
Bows to the rushing wind its glorious head,
The universal arch of yonder spheres
Sunk with the pressure of its Maker's tread,
And earth's foundations quaked with mortal fears.

SONNET.

THE CRUCIFIXION.

IMITATED FROM THE ITALIAN OF CRESCIMBENI.

I ASK'D the Heavens, — "What foe to GOD hath done
This unexampled deed?" — The Heavens exclaim,
"'T was Man; — and we in horror snatch'd the sun
From such a spectacle of guilt and shame."

I ask'd the Sea; — the Sea in fury boil'd,
And answer'd with his voice of storms, "'T was Man:
My waves in panic at his crime recoil'd,
Disclosed the' abyss, and from the centre ran."

I ask'd the Earth; — the Earth replied aghast,
"'T was Man; — and such strange pangs my bosom rent,
That still I groan and shudder at the past."
— To Man, gay, smiling, thoughtless Man, I went,
And ask'd him next: — *He* turn'd a scornful eye,
Shook his proud head, and deign'd me no reply.

THE BIBLE.

WHAT is the world! — A wildering maze,
Where Sin hath track'd ten thousand ways,
Her victims to ensnare;
All broad, and winding, and aslope,
All tempting with perfidious hope,
All ending in despair.

Millions of pilgrims throng those roads,
Bearing their baubles, or their loads,
Down to eternal night;
— *One* humble path, that never bends,
Narrow, and rough, and steep, ascends
From darkness into light.

Is there a Guide to show that path?
The Bible: — He alone who hath
The Bible, need not stray:
Yet he who hath, and will not give
That heavenly Guide to all that live,
Himself shall lose the way.

INSTRUCTION.

From heaven descend the drops of dew,
From heaven the gracious showers,
Earth's winter-aspect to renew,
And clothe the spring with flowers ;
From heaven the beams of morning flow,
That melt the gloom of night ;
From heaven the evening breezes blow,
Health, fragrance, and delight.

Like genial dew, like fertile showers,
The words of wisdom fall,
Awaken man's unconscious powers,
Strength out of weakness call :
Like morning beams they strike the mind,
Its loveliness reveal ;
And softer than the evening wind
The wounded spirit heal.

As dew and rain, as light and air,
From heaven Instruction came,
The waste of Nature to repair,
Kindle a sacred flame ;
A flame to purify the earth,
Exalt her sons on high,

And train them for their second birth,
— Their birth beyond the sky.

Albion! on every human soul,
By thee be knowledge shed,
Far as the ocean-waters roll,
Wide as the shores are spread:
Truth makes thy children free at home;
Oh! that thy flag, unfurl'd,
Might shine, where'er thy children roam,
Truth's banner round the world.

London, 1812.

THE CHRISTIAN SOLDIER.

OCCASIONED BY THE SUDDEN DEATH OF THE

REV. THOMAS TAYLOR;

After having declared, in his last Sermon, on a preceding evening, that he hoped to die as an old soldier of Jesus Christ, with his sword in his hand.

"Servant of God! well done,
Rest from thy loved employ;
The battle fought, the victory won,
Enter thy Master's joy."
— The voice at midnight came;
He started up to hear:
A mortal arrow pierced his frame,
He fell, — but felt no fear.

Tranquil amidst alarms,
It found him in the field,
A veteran slumbering on his arms,
Beneath his red-cross shield:
His sword was in his hand,
Still warm with recent fight,
Ready that moment at command,
Through rock and steel to smite.

It was a two-edged blade,
Of heavenly temper keen:
And double were the wounds it made,
Where'er it smote between:
'T was death to sin; — 't was life
To all that mourn'd for sin;
It kindled and it silenced strife,
Made war and peace within.

Oft with its fiery force,
His arm had quell'd the foe,
And laid, resistless in his course,
The alien-armies low:
Bent on such glorious toils,
The world to him was loss;
Yet all his trophies, all his spoils,
He hung upon the cross.

At midnight came the cry,
"To meet thy God prepare!"
He woke, and caught his Captain's eye;
Then strong in faith and prayer,
His spirit, with a bound,
Bursts its encumbering clay:
His tent, at sunrise, on the ground,
A darken'd ruin lay.

The pains of death are past,
Labor and sorrow cease,
And life's long warfare closed at last,
His soul is found in peace.

Soldier of Christ! well done;
Praise be thy new employ;
And while eternal ages run,
Rest in thy Saviour's joy.

ON THE ROYAL INFANT,

STILL-BORN, NOV. 5, 1817.

A THRONE on earth awaited thee;
A nation long'd to see thy face,
Heir to a glorious ancestry,
And father of a mightier race.

Vain hope! that throne thou must not fill;
Thee may that nation ne'er behold;
Thine ancient house is heirless still,
Thy line shall never be unroll'd.

Yet while we mourn thy flight from earth,
Thine was a destiny sublime;
Caught up to Paradise in birth,
Pluck'd by Eternity from Time.

The mother knew her offspring dead:
Oh! was it grief, or was it love
That broke her heart?—The spirit fled
To seek her nameless child above.

Led by his natal star, she trod
The path to heaven:—the meeting there,
And how they stood before their GOD,
The day of judgment shall declare.

A MIDNIGHT THOUGHT.

In a land of strange delight,
My transported spirit stray'd;
I awake where all is night,
Silence, solitude, and shade.

Is the dream of Nature flown?
Is the universe destroy'd,
Man extinct, and I alone
Breathing through the formless void?

No:— my soul, in God rejoice!
Through the gloom his light I see,
In the silence hear his voice,
And his hand is over me.

When I slumber in the tomb,
He will guard my resting-place:
Fearless in the day of doom,
May I stand before his face!

A NIGHT IN A STAGE-COACH;

BEING A MEDITATION ON THE WAY BETWEEN LONDON AND BRISTOL,

SEPTEMBER 23, 1815.

I TRAVEL all the irksome night,
  By ways to me unknown;
I travel, like a bird in flight,
  Onward, and all alone.

In vain I close my weary eyes,
  They will not, cannot sleep,
But, like the watchers of the skies,
  Their twinkling vigils keep.

My thoughts are wandering wild and far;
  From earth to heaven they dart;
Now wing their flight from star to star,
  Now dive into my heart.

Backward they roll the tide of time,
  And live through vanish'd years,
Or hold their "colloquy sublime"
  With future hopes and fears;

Then passing joys and present woes
  Chase through my troubled mind,
Repose still seeking, — but repose
  Not for a moment find.

So yonder lone and lovely moon
  Gleams on the clouds gone by,
Illumines those around her noon,
  Yet westward points her eye.

Nor wind nor flood her course delay.
  Through heaven I see her glide;
She never pauses on her way
  She never turns aside.

With anxious heart and throbbing brain,
  Strength, patience, spirits gone,
Pulses of fire in every vein,
  Thus, thus I journey on.

But soft! — in Nature's failing hour,
  Up springs a breeze, — I feel
Its balmy breath, its cordial power,
  — A power to soothe and heal.

Lo! grey, and gold, and crimson streaks
  The gorgeous east adorn,
While o'er the' empurpled mountain breaks
  The glory of the morn.

Insensibly the stars retire,
  Exhaled like drops of dew;
Now through an arch of living fire,
  The sun comes forth to view.

The hills, the vales, the waters burn
  With his enkindling rays,
No sooner touch'd than they return
  A tributary blaze.

His quickening light on me descends,
  His cheering warmth I own;
Upward to him my spirit tends,
  But worships GOD alone.

Oh! that on me, with beams benign,
  His countenance would turn:
I too should then arise and shine,
  — Arise, and shine, and burn.

Slowly I raise my languid head,
  Pain and soul-sickness cease;
The phantoms of dismay are fled,
  And health returns, and peace.

Where is the beauty of the scene,
  Which silent night display'd?
The clouds, the stars, the blue serene,
  The moving light and shade?

All gone! — the moon, erewhile so bright,
Veil'd with a dusky shroud,
Seems, in the sun's o'erpowering light,
The fragment of a cloud.

At length, I reach my journey's end:
— Welcome that well-known face!
I meet a brother and a friend;
I find a resting-place.

Just such a pilgrimage is life;
Hurried from stage to stage,
Our wishes with our lot at strife,
Through childhood to old age.

The world is seldom what it seems. —
To man, who dimly sees,
Realities appear as dreams,
And dreams realities.

The Christian's years, though slow their flight,
When he is call'd away,
Are but the watches of a night,
And Death the dawn of day.

THE REIGN OF SPRING.

Who loves not Spring's voluptuous hours,
The carnival of birds and flowers?
Yet who would choose, however dear,
That Spring should revel all the year?
— Who loves not Summer's splendid reign,
The bridal of the earth and main?
Yet who would choose, however bright,
A Dog-day noon without a night?
— Who loves not Autumn's joyous round,
When corn, and wine, and oil abound?
Yet who would choose, however gay,
A year of unrenew'd decay?
— Who loves not Winter's awful form?
The sphere-born music of the storm?
Yet who would choose, how grand soever,
The shortest day to last for ever?

'T was in that age renown'd, remote,
When all was true that Esop wrote;
And in that land of fair Ideal,
Where all that poets dream is real;
Upon a day of annual state,
The Seasons met in high debate.
There blush'd young Spring in maiden pride,
Blithe Summer look'd a gorgeous bride,

Staid Autumn moved with matron-grace,
And beldame Winter pursed her face.
Dispute grew wild; all talk'd together;
The four at once made wondrous weather;
Nor one (whate'er the rest had shown)
Heard any reason but her own,
While each (for nothing else was clear)
Claim'd the whole circle of the year.

Spring, in possession of the field,
Compell'd her sisters soon to yield:
They part, — resolved elsewhere to try
A twelvemonth's empire of the sky;
And, calling off their airy legions,
Alighted in adjacent regions.
Spring o'er the eastern champaign smiled,
Fell Winter ruled the northern wild,
Summer pursued the sun's red car,
But Autumn loved the twilight star.

As Spring parades her new domain,
Love, Beauty, Pleasure, hold her train;
Her footsteps wake the flowers beneath,
That start, and blush, and sweetly breathe;
Her gales on nimble pinions rove,
And shake to foliage every grove;
Her voice, in dell and thicket heard,
Cheers on the nest the mother-bird;
The ice-lock'd streams, as if they felt
Her touch, to liquid diamond melt;

The lambs around her bleat and play;
The serpent flings his slough away,
And shines in orient colors dight,
A flexile ray of living light.
Nature unbinds her wintry shroud
(As the soft sunshine melts the cloud),
With infant gambols sports along,
Bounds into youth, and soars in song.
The morn impearls her locks with dew,
Noon spreads a sky of boundless blue,
The rainbow spans the evening scene,
The night is silent and serene,
Save when her lonely minstrel wrings
The heart with sweetness while he sings.
— Who would not wish, unrivall'd here,
That Spring might frolic all the year?

Three months are fled, and still she reigns,
Exulting queen o'er hills and plains;
The birds renew their nuptial vow,
Nestlings themselves are lovers now;
Fresh broods each bending bough receives,
Till feathers far outnumber leaves;
But kites in circles swim the air,
And sadden music to despair.
The stagnant pools, the quaking bogs,
Teem, croak, and crawl with hordes of frogs;
The matted woods, the' infected earth,
Are venomous with reptile-birth;
Armies of locusts cloud the skies;
With beetles hornets, gnats with flies,

Interminable warfare wage,
And madden heaven with insect-rage.

The flowers are wither'd; — sun nor dew
Their fallen glories shall renew;
The flowers are wither'd; — germ nor seed
Ripen in garden, wild, or mead:
The corn-fields shoot: — their blades, alas!
Run riot in luxuriant grass.
The tainted flocks, the drooping kine,
In famine of abundance pine,
Where vegetation, sour, unsound,
And loathsome, rots and rankles round;
Nature with nature seems at strife;
Nothing can live but monstrous life
By death engender'd; — food and breath
Are turn'd to elements of death;
And where the soil his victims strew,
Corruption quickens them anew.

But ere the year was half expired,
Spring saw her folly, and retired;
Yoked her light chariot to a breeze,
And mounted to the Pleiades;
Content with them to rest or play
Along the calm nocturnal way;
Till, heaven's remaining circuit run,
They meet the pale hybernal sun,
And, gaily mingling in his blaze,
Hail the true dawn of vernal days.

THE REIGN OF SUMMER.

The hurricanes are fled; the rains,
That plough'd the mountains, wreck'd the plains,
Have pass'd away before the wind,
And left a wilderness behind,
As if an ocean had been there
Exhaled, and left its channels bare.
But, with a new and sudden birth,
Nature replenishes the earth;
Plants, flowers, and shrubs, o'er all the land
So promptly rise, so thickly stand,
As if they heard a voice, — and came,
Each at the calling of its name.
The tree, by tempests stript and rent,
Expands its verdure like a tent,
Beneath whose shade, in weary length,
The' enormous lion rests his strength,
For blood, in dreams of hunting, burns,
Or, chased himself, to fight returns;
Growls in his sleep, a dreary sound,
Grinds his wedged teeth, and spurns the ground:
While monkeys, in grotesque amaze,
Down from their bending perches gaze,
But when he lifts his eye of fire,
Quick to the topmost boughs retire.

Loud o'er the mountains bleat the flocks;
The goat is bounding on the rocks;
Far in the valleys range the herds;
The welkin gleams with flitting birds,
Whose plumes such gorgeous tints adorn,
They seem the offspring of the morn.
From nectar'd flowers and groves of spice,
Earth breathes the air of Paradise;
Her mines their hidden wealth betray,
Treasures of darkness burst to day;
O'er golden sands the rivers glide,
And pearls and amber track the tide.
Of every sensual bliss possess'd,
Man riots here; — but *is* he bless'd?
And would he choose, for ever bright,
This Summer-day without a night?
For here hath Summer fix'd her throne,
Intent to reign, — and reign alone.

Daily the sun, in his career,
Hotter and higher, climbs the sphere,
Till from the zenith, in his rays,
Without a cloud or shadow, blaze
The realms beneath him: — in his march,
On the blue key-stone of heaven's arch,
He stands; — air, earth, and ocean lie
Within the presence of his eye.
The wheel of Nature seems to rest,
Nor rolls him onward to the west,

Till thrice three days of noon unchanged,
That torrid clime have so deranged,
Nine years may not the wrong repair;
But summer checks the ravage there;
Yet still enjoins the sun to steer
By the stern Dog-star round the year,
With dire extremes of day and night,
Tartarean gloom, celestial light.

In vain the gaudy season shines,
Her beauty fades, her power declines;
Then first her bosom felt a care;
— No healing breeze embalm'd the air,
No mist the mountain-tops bedew'd,
Nor shower the arid vale renew'd;
The herbage shrunk: the ploughman's toil
Scatter'd to dust the crumbling soil;
Blossoms were shed; the' umbrageous wood,
Laden with sapless foliage, stood;
The streams, impoverish'd day by day,
Lessen'd insensibly away;
Where cattle sought, with piteous moans,
The vanish'd lymph, midst burning stones,
And tufts of wither'd reeds, that fill
The wonted channel of the rill;
Till, stung with hornets, mad with thirst,
In sudden rout, away they burst,
Nor rest, till where some channel deep
Gleams in small pools, whose waters sleep;

There with huge draught and eager eye
Drink for existence, — drink and die!

But direr evils soon arose,
Hopeless, unmitigable woes;
Man proves the shock; through all his veins
The frenzy of the season reigns;
With pride, lust, rage, ambition blind,
He burns in every fire of mind,
Which kindles from insane desire,
Or fellest hatred can inspire;
Reckless whatever ill befall,
He dares to do and suffer all
That heart can think, that arm can deal,
Or out of hell a fury feel.

There stood in that romantic clime,
A mountain awfully sublime;
O'er many a league the basement spread,
It tower'd in many an airy head,
Height over height, — now gay, now wild,
The peak with ice eternal piled;
Pure in mid-heaven, that crystal cone
A diadem of glory shone,
Reflecting, in the night-fall'n sky,
The beams of day's departed eye;
Or holding, ere the dawn begun,
Communion with the' unrisen sun.
The cultured sides were clothed with woods,
Vineyards, and fields; or track'd with floods,

Whose glacier fountains, hid on high,
Sent down their rivers from the sky.
O'er plains, that mark'd its gradual scale,
On sunny slope, in shelter'd vale,
Earth's universal tenant, — He,
Who lives wherever life may be,
Sole, social, fix'd, or free to roam,
Always and everywhere at home,
MAN pitch'd his tents, adorn'd his bowers,
Built temples, palaces, and towers,
And made that Alpine world his own,
— The miniature of every zone,
From brown savannas parch'd below,
To ridges of cerulean snow.

Those high-lands form'd a last retreat
From rapid Summer's fatal heat:
Though not unfelt her fervors there,
Vernal and cool the middle air;
While from the icy pyramid
Streams of unfailing freshness slid,
That long had slaked the thirsty land,
Till avarice, with insatiate hand,
Their currents check'd; in sunless caves,
And rock-bound dells, ingulf'd the waves,
And thence in scanty measures doled,
Or turn'd heaven's bounty into gold.
Ere long the dwellers on the plain
Murmur'd, — their murmurs were in vain;

Petition'd, — but their prayers were spurn'd;
Threaten'd, — defiance was return'd;
Then rang both regions with alarms;
Blood-kindling trumpets blew to arms;
The maddening drum and deafening fife
Marshall'd the elements of strife:
Sternly the mountaineers maintain
Their rights against the' insurgent plain;
The plain's indignant myriads rose
To wrest the mountain from their foes,
Resolved its blessings to enjoy
By dint of valor, — or destroy.

The legions met in war-array;
The mountaineers brook'd no delay;
Aside their missile weapons threw,
From holds impregnable withdrew,
And, rashly brave, with sword and shield,
Rush'd headlong to the open field.
Their foes the' auspicious omen took,
And raised a battle-shout that shook
The champaign; — stanch and keen for blood,
Front threatening front, the columns stood;
But, while like thunder-clouds they frown,
In tropic haste the sun went down;
Night o'er both armies stretch'd her tent,
The star-bespangled firmament,
Whose placid host, revolving slow,
Smile on the' impatient hordes below,

That chafe and fret the hours away,
Curse the dull gloom, and long for day,
Though destined by their own decree
No other day nor night to see.
— That night is past, that day begun;
Swift as he sunk ascends the sun,
And from the red horizon springs
Upward, as borne on eagle-wings:
Aslant each army's lengthen'd lines,
O'er shields and helms he proudly shines,
While spears, that catch his lightnings keen,
Flash them athwart the space between.
Before the battle-shock, when breath
And pulse are still, — awaiting death;
In that cold pause, which seems to be
The prelude to eternity,
When fear, e'er yet a blow is dealt,
Betray'd by none, by all is felt;
While, moved beneath their feet, the tomb
Widens her lap to make them room;
— Till, in the onset of the fray,
Fear, feeling, thought are cast away,
And foaming, raging, mingling foes,
Like billows dash'd in conflict, close,
Charge, strike, repel, wound, struggle, fly,
Gloriously win, unconquer'd die: —
Here in dread silence, while they stand,
Each with a death-stroke in his hand,
His eye fix'd forward, and his ear
Tingling the signal blast to hear;

The trumpet sounds; — one note, — no more;
The field, the fight, the war is o'er;
An earthquake rent the void between;
A moment show'd, and shut the scene;
Men, chariots, steeds, — of either host,
The flower, the pride, the strength were lost:
A solitude remains; — the dead
Are buried there, — the living fled.

Nor yet the reign of Summer closed;
— At night in their own homes reposed
The fugitives, on either side,
Who 'scaped the death their comrades died;
When, lo! with many a giddy shock
The mountain-cliffs began to rock,
And deep below the hollow ground
Ran a strange mystery of sound,
As if, in chains and torments there,
Spirits were venting their despair.
That sound, those shocks, the sleepers woke;
In trembling consternation, broke
Forth from their dwellings, young and old;
— Nothing abroad their eyes behold
But darkness so intensely wrought,
'Twas blindness in themselves they thought.
Anon, aloof, with sudden rays,
Issued so fierce, so broad a blaze,
That darkness started into light,
And every eye, restored to sight,

Gazed on the glittering crest of snows,
Whence the bright conflagration rose,
Whose flames condensed at once aspire,
— A pillar of celestial fire,
Alone amidst infernal shade,
In glorious majesty display'd:
Beneath, from rifted caverns, broke
Volumes of suffocating smoke,
That roll'd in surges, like a flood,
By the red radiance turn'd to blood;
Morn look'd aghast upon the scene,
Nor could a sunbeam pierce between
The panoply of vapors, spread
Above, around the mountain's head.

In distant fields, with drought consumed,
Joy swell'd all hearts, all eyes illumed,
When from that peak, through lowering skies,
Thick curling clouds were seen to rise,
And hang o'er all the darken'd plain,
The presage of descending rain.
The' exulting cattle bound along,
The tuneless birds attempt a song,
The swain, amidst his sterile lands,
With outstretch'd arms of rapture stands.
But, fraught with plague and curses, came
The' insidious progeny of flame;
Ah! then, — for fertilizing showers,
The pledge of herbage, fruits, and flowers, —

Words cannot paint, how every eye
(Blood-shot and dim with agony)
Was glazed, as by a palsying spell,
When light sulphureous ashes fell,
Dazzling, and eddying to and fro,
Like wildering sleet or feathery snow:
Strewn with grey pumice Nature lies,
At every motion quick to rise,
Tainting with livid fumes the air;
— Then hope lies down in prone despair,
And man and beast, with misery dumb,
Sullenly brood on woes to come.

The mountain now, like living earth,
Pregnant with some stupendous birth,
Heaved, in the anguish of its throes,
Sheer from its crest the' incumbent snows;
And where of old they chill'd the sky,
Beneath the sun's meridian eye,
Or, purpling in the golden west,
Appear'd his evening throne of rest,
There, black and bottomless and wide,
A cauldron, rent from side to side,
Simmer'd and hiss'd with huge turmoil;
Earth's disembowell'd minerals boil,
And thence in molten torrents rush:
— Water and fire, like sisters, gush
From the same source; the double stream
Meets, battles, and explodes in steam;
Then fire prevails; and broad and deep
Red lava roars from steep to steep;

While rocks unseated, woods upriven,
Are headlong down the current driven;
Columnar flames are wrapt aloof,
In whirlwind forms, to heaven's high roof,
And there, amidst transcendent gloom,
Image the wrath beyond the tomb.

The mountaineers, in wild affright,
Too late for safety, urge their flight;
Women, made childless in the fray,
Women, made mothers yesterday,
The sick, the aged, and the blind;
— None but the dead are left behind.
Painful their journey, toilsome, slow,
Beneath their feet quick embers glow,
And hurtle round in dreadful hail;
Their limbs, their hearts, their senses fail,
While many a victim, by the way,
Buried alive in ashes lay,
Or perish'd by the lightning's stroke,
Before the slower thunder broke.
A few the open field explore:
The throng seek refuge on the shore,
Between two burning rivers hemm'd,
Whose rage nor mounds nor hollows stemm'd;
Driven like a herd of deer, they reach
The lonely, dark, and silent beach,
Where, calm as innocence in sleep,
Expanded lies the' unconscious deep.
Awhile the fugitives respire,
And watch those cataracts of fire

(That bar escape on either hand)
Rush on the ocean from the strand;
Back from the onset rolls the tide,
But instant clouds the conflict hide;
The lavas plunge to gulfs unknown,
And, as they plunge, collapse to stone.

Meanwhile the mad volcano grew
Tenfold more terrible to view;
And thunders, such as shall be hurl'd
At the death-sentence of the world;
And lightnings, such as shall consume
Creation, and creation's tomb,
Nor leave, amidst the' eternal void,
One trembling atom undestroy'd;
Such thunders crash'd, such lightnings glared:
— Another fate those outcasts shared,
When, with one desolating sweep,
An earthquake seem'd to' ingulf the deep,
Then threw it back, and from its bed
Hung a whole ocean overhead;
The victims shriek'd beneath the wave,
And in a moment found one grave;
Down to the' abyss the flood return'd —
Alone, unseen, the mountain burn'd.

1815.

INCOGNITA:

ON VIEWING THE PICTURE OF AN UNKNOWN LADY.

WRITTEN AT LEAMINGTON, IN 1817.

"She was a phantom of delight." WORDSWORTH.

IMAGE of One, who lived of yore!
  Hail to that lovely mien,
Once quick and conscious, — now no more
  On land or ocean seen!
Were all earth's breathing forms to pass
Before me in Agrippa's glass,*
Many as fair as Thou might be,
But oh! not one, — not one like Thee.

Thou art no Child of Fancy; — Thou
  The very look dost wear,
That gave enchantment to a brow,
  Wreathed with luxuriant hair;

* Henry Cornelius Agrippa, of Nettesheim, counsellor to Charles V. Emperor of Germany, — the author of "Occult Philosophy," and other profound works, — is said to have shown to the Earl of Surrey the image of his mistress Geraldine in a magical mirror.

Lips of the morn embathed in dew,
And eyes of evening's starry blue;
Of all who e'er enjoy'd the sun,
Thou art the image of but *One.*

And who was she, in virgin prime,
  And May of womanhood,
Whose roses here, unpluck'd by Time,
  In shadowy tints have stood;
While many a winter's withering blast
Hath o'er the dark cold chamber pass'd,
In which her once resplendent form
Slumber'd to dust beneath the storm?

Of gentle blood; — upon her birth
  Consenting planets smiled,
And she had seen those days of mirth
  That frolic round the child;
To bridal bloom her strength had sprung,
Behold her beautiful and young!
Lives there a record, which hath told
That she was wedded, widow'd, old?

How long her date, 'twere vain to guess:
  The pencil's cunning art
Can but a single glance express,
  One motion of the heart;
A smile, a blush, — a transient grace
Of air, and attitude, and face;
One passion's changing color mix,
One moment's flight for ages fix.

Her joys and griefs alike in vain
  Would fancy here recall;
Her throbs of ecstasy or pain
  Lull'd in oblivion all;
With her, methinks, life's little hour
Pass'd like the fragrance of a flower,
That leaves upon the vernal wind
Sweetness we ne'er again may find.

Where dwelt she?—Ask yon aged tree,
  Whose boughs embower the lawn,
Whether the birds' wild minstrelsy
  Awoke her here at dawn?
Whether beneath its youthful shade,
At noon, in infancy she play'd?
—If from the oak no answer come,
Of her all oracles are dumb.

The Dead are like the stars by day;
  —Withdrawn from mortal eye,
But not extinct, they hold their way
  In glory through the sky:
Spirits, from bondage thus set free,
Vanish amidst immensity,
Where human thought, like human sight,
Fails to pursue their trackless flight.

Somewhere within created space,
  Could I explore that round,
In bliss, or woe, there is a place
  Where she might still be found;

And oh! unless those eyes deceive,
I may, I must, I will believe,
That she, whose charms so meekly glow,
Is what she only seem'd below ;—

An angel in that glorious realm
   Where God himself is King:
— But awe and fear, that overwhelm
   Presumption, check my wing;
Nor dare imagination look
Upon the symbols of that book,
Wherein eternity enrolls
The judgments on departed souls.

Of Her of whom these pictured lines
   A faint resemblance form;
— Fair as the *second* rainbow shines
   Aloof amid the storm ;
Of her, this "shadow of a shade,"
Like its original, must fade,
And She, forgotten when unseen,
Shall be as if she ne'er had been.

Ah! then, perchance, this dreaming strain,
   Of all that e'er I sung,
A lorn memorial may remain,
   When silent lies my tongue ;
When shot the meteor of my fame,
Lost the vain echo of my name,
This leaf, this fallen leaf, may be
The only trace of her and me.

With One who lived of old, my song
  In lowly cadence rose;
To One who is unborn, belong
  The accents of its close:
Ages to come, with courteous ear,
Some youth my warning voice may hear;
And voices from the dead should be
The warnings of eternity.

When these weak lines thy presence greet,
  Reader! if I am bless'd,
Again, as spirits, may we meet
  In glory and in rest!
If not, — and *I* have lost my way,
Here part we, — go not *Thou* astray:
No tomb, no verse my story tell;
Once, and for ever, Fare Thee well!

THE LITTLE CLOUD.

Seen in a country excursion, among the woods and rocks of Wharncliffe and the adjacent park and pleasure grounds of Wortley Hall, the seat of the Right Honorable Lord Wharncliffe, near Sheffield, on the 30th day of June, 1818.

The summer sun was in the west,
Yet far above his evening rest;
A thousand clouds in air display'd
Their floating isles of light and shade,
The sky, like ocean's channels, seen
In long meandering streaks between.

Cultured and waste, the landscape lay,
Woods, mountains, valleys stretch'd away,
And throng'd the' immense horizon round,
With heaven's eternal girdle bound;
From inland towns, eclipsed with smoke,
Steeples in lonely grandeur broke;
Hamlets, and cottages, and streams
By glimpses caught the casual gleams,
Or blazed in lustre broad and strong,
Beyond the picturing powers of song:
O'er all the eye enchanted ranged,
While colors, forms, proportions changed,
Or sunk in distance undefined,

Still as our devious course inclined,
— And oft we paused, and look'd behind.

One little cloud, and only one,
Seem'd the pure offspring of the sun,
Flung from his orb to show us here
What clouds adorn *his* hemisphere:
Unmoved, unchanging, in the gale,
That bore the rest o'er hill and dale,
Whose shadowy shapes, with lights around,
Like living motions, swept the ground,
This little cloud, and this alone,
Long in the highest ether shone;
Gay as a warrior's banner spread,
Its sunward margin ruby-red,
Green, purple, gold, and every hue
That glitters in the morning dew,
Or glows along the rainbow's form,
— The apparition of the storm.
Deep in its bosom, diamond-bright,
Behind a fleece of pearly white,
It seemed a secret glory dwelt,
Whose presence, while unseen, was felt;
Like Beauty's eye, in slumber hid
Beneath a half-transparent lid,
From whence a sound, a touch, a breath,
Might startle it, — as life from death.

Looks, words, emotions of surprise
Welcomed the stranger to our eyes:

Was it the phœnix, that from earth
In flames of incense sprang to birth?
Had ocean from his lap let fly
His loveliest halcyon through the sky?
No: — while we gazed, the pageant grew
A nobler object to our view;
We deem'd, if heaven with earth would hold
Communion, as in days of old,
Such, on his journey down the sphere,
Benignant RAPHAEL might appear,
In splendid mystery conceal'd,
Yet by his rich disguise reveal'd:
— That buoyant vapor, in mid-air,
An angel in its folds might bear,
Who, through the curtain of his shrine,
Betray'd his lineaments divine.
The wild, the warm illusion stole,
Like inspiration, o'er the soul,
Till thought was rapture, language hung
Silent but trembling on the tongue;
And fancy almost hoped to hail
The seraph rushing through his veil,
Or hear an awful voice proclaim
The embassy on which he came.

But ah! no minister of grace
Show'd from the firmament his face,
Nor, borne aloof on balanced wings,
Reveal'd unutterable things.
The sun went down: — the vision pass'd;
The cloud was *but* a cloud at last;

Yet, when its brilliancy decay'd,
The eye still linger'd on the shade,
And watching, till no longer seen,
Loved it for what it once had been.

That cloud was beautiful, — was one
Among a thousand round the sun;
The thousand shared the common lot;
They came, — they went, — they were forgot;
This fairy-form alone impress'd
Its perfect image in my breast,
And shines as richly blazon'd there
As in its element of air.

The day on which that cloud appear'd,
Exhilarating scenes endear'd:
— The sunshine on the hills, the floods;
The breeze, the twilight of the woods;
Nature in every change of green,
Heaven in unnumber'd aspects seen;
Health, spirits, exercise, release
From noise and smoke; twelve hours of peace;
No fears to haunt, no cares to vex;
Friends, young and old, of either sex;
Converse familiar, sportive, kind,
Where heart meets heart, mind quickens mind,
And words and thoughts are all at play,
Like children on a holiday;
— Till themes celestial rapt the soul
In adoration o'er the pole,

Where stars are darkness in *His* sight,
Who reigns invisible in light,
High above all created things,
The Lord of Lords, the King of Kings!
Faith, which could thus on wing sublime
Outsoar the bounded flight of time;
Hope full of immortality,
And GOD in all the eye could see;
— These, these endear'd that day to me,
And made it, in a thousand ways,
A day among a thousand days,
That share with clouds the common lot;
They come, — they go, — they are forgot:
This, like that plaything of the sun,
— The little, lonely, lovely one,
This lives within me; this shall be
A part of my eternity.

Amidst the cares, the toils, the strife,
The weariness and waste of life,
That day shall memory oft restore,
And in a moment live it o'er,
When, with a lightning-flash of thought,
Morn, noon, and eve at once are brought
(As through the vision of a trance)
All in the compass of a glance.

Oh! should I reach a world above,
And sometimes think of those I love,

Of things on earth too dearly prized
(Nor yet by saints in heaven despised),
Though Spirits made perfect may lament
Life's holier hours as half mis-spent,
Methinks I could not turn away
The fond remembrance of that day,
The bright idea of that cloud
(Survivor of a countless crowd),
Without a pause, perhaps a sigh,
To think such loveliness should die,
And clouds and days of storm and gloom
Scowl on Man's passage to the tomb.
— Not so : — I feel I have a heart
Blessings to share, improve, impart,
In blithe, severe, or pensive mood,
At home, abroad, in solitude,
Whatever clouds are on the wing,
Whatever day the seasons bring.

That is true happiness below,
Which conscience cannot turn to woe;
And though such happiness depends
Neither on clouds, nor days, nor friends,
When friends, and days, and clouds unite,
And kindred chords are tuned aright,
The harmonies of heaven and earth,
Through eye, ear, intellect, give birth
To joys too exquisite to last,
— And yet *more* exquisite when past!

When the soul summons by a spell
The ghosts of pleasures round her cell,
In saintlier forms than erst they wore,
And smiles benigner than before,
Each loved, lamented, scene renews
With warmer touches, tenderer hues;
Recalls kind words forever flown,
But echoed in a soften'd tone;
Wakes, with new pulses in the breast,
Feelings forgotten or at rest;
— The thought how fugitive and fair,
How dear and precious such things were!
That thought, with gladness more refined,
Deep and transporting, thrills the mind,
Than all those pleasures of an hour,
When most the soul confess'd their power.

Bliss in possession will not last;
Remember'd joys are never past;
At once the fountain, stream, and sea,
They were, — they are, — they yet shall be.

ABDALLAH AND SABAT.*

[Originally published with "Abdallah, or the Christian Martyr," by Thomas Foster Barham, Esq.]

FROM West Arabia to Bochara came
A noble youth, Abdallah was his name;
Who journey'd through the various East to find
New forms of man, in feature, habit, mind;
Where Tartar-hordes through nature's pastures run,
A race of Centaurs, — horse and rider one;
Where the soft Persian maid the breath inhales
Of love-sick roses, woo'd by nightingales;
Where India's grim array of idols seem
The rabble-phantoms of a maniac's dream:
— Himself the flowery path of trespass trod,
Which the false Prophet deck'd to lure from GOD.
But He, who changed, into the faith of Paul,
The slaughter-breathing enmity of Saul,
Vouchsafed to meet Abdallah by the way:
No miracle of light eclipsed the day;
No vision from the' eternal world, nor sound
Of awe and wonder smote him to the ground;

* See Buchanan's "Christian Researches in India," for the martyrdom of Abdallah, and the conversion and labors of Sabat. "The Christian Observer," February, 1818, contains the account of Sabat's dreadful fate.

All mild and calm, with power till then unknown,
The gospel-glory through his darkness shone;
A still small whisper, only heard within,
Convinced the trembling penitent of sin;
And Jesus, whom the Infidel abhorr'd,
The Convert now invoked, and call'd him Lord.
Escaping from the lewd Impostor's snare,
As flits a bird released through boundless air,
And, soaring up the pure blue ether, sings,
— So rose his Spirit on exulting wings.
But love, joy, peace, the Christian's bliss below,
Are deeply mingled in a cup of woe,
Which none can pass: — he, counting all things loss
For his Redeemer, gladly bore the cross:
Soon call'd, with life, to lay that burden down,
In the first fight he won the Martyr's crown.

Abdallah's friend was Sabat; — one of those
Whom love estranged transforms to bitterest foes:
From persecution to that friend he fled;
But Sabat pour'd reproaches on his head,
Spurn'd like a leprous plague the prostrate youth,
And hated him as falsehood hates the truth;
Yet first with sophistry and menace tried
To turn him from "the faithful word" aside;
All failing, old esteem to rancor turn'd,
With Mahomet's own reckless rage he burn'd.
A thousand hideous thoughts, like fiends, possess'd
The Pandemonium of the Bigot's breast,
Whose fires, enkindled from the' infernal lake,
Abdallah's veins, unsluiced, alone could slake.

The victim, dragg'd to slaughter by his friend,
Witness'd a good confession to the end.
Bochara pour'd her people forth, to gaze
Upon the direst scene the world displays,
The blood of innocence by treason spilt,
The reeking triumph of deep-branded guilt:
— Bochara pour'd her people forth, to eye
The loveliest spectacle beneath the sky,
The look with which a Martyr yields his breath,
— The resurrection of the soul in death.
"Renounce the Nazarene!" the headsman cries,
And flash'd the unstain'd falchion in his eyes:
"No! — be his name by heaven and earth adored!"
He said, and gave his right hand to the sword.
"Renounce Him, who forsakes thee thus bereft;"
He wept, but spake not, and resign'd his left.
"Renounce Him now, who will not, cannot save;"
He kneel'd, like Stephen, look'd beyond the grave,
And, while the dawn of heaven around him broke,
Bow'd his meek head to the dissevering stroke:
Outcast on earth a mangled body lay;
A spirit enter'd Paradise that day.

But where is Sabat? — Conscience-struck he stands,
With eye of agony, and fast-lock'd hands.
Abdallah, in the moment to depart,
Had turn'd, and look'd the traitor through the heart:
It smote him like a judgment from above,
That gentle look of wrong'd, forgiving love!

Then hatred vanish'd; suddenly repress'd
Were the strange flames of passion in his breast;
Nought but the smouldering ashes of despair,
Blackness of darkness, death of death, were there.
Ere long, wild whirlwinds of remorse arise;
He flies, — from all except himself he flies,
And a low voice for ever thrilling near,
The voice of blood which none but he can hear.

He fled from guilt; but guilt and he were one,
A Spirit seeking rest and finding none;
Visions of horror haunted him by night,
Yet darkness was less terrible than light;
From dreams of woe when startled nature broke,
To woes that were not dreams the wretch awoke.
Forlorn he ranged through India, till the Power,
That met Abdallah in a happier hour,
Arrested Sabat: through his soul he felt
The word of truth; his heart began to melt,
And yielded slowly, as cold Winter yields
When the warm Spring comes flushing o'er the fields;
Then first a tear of gladness swell'd his eye,
Then first his bosom heaved a healthful sigh;
That bosom, parch'd as Afric's desert land;
That eye, a flint-stone in the burning sand.
— Peace, pardon, hope, eternal joy, reveal'd,
Humbled his heart: before the cross he kneel'd,
Look'd up to Him whom once he pierced, and bore
The name of Christ which he blasphemed before.
— Was Sabat then subdued by love or fear?
And who shall vouch that he was not sincere?

Now with a Convert's zeal his ardent mind
Glow'd for the common weal of all mankind;
Yet with intenser faith the' Arabian pray'd,
When homeward thought thro' childhood's Eden stray'd.
— There, in the lap of Yemen's happiest vale,
The shepherd's tents are waving to the gale;
The Patriarch of their tribe, his sire, he sees
Beneath the shadow of ambrosial trees;
His Sisters, from the fountain in the rock,
Pour the cool sparkling water to their flock;
His Brethren, rapt on steeds and camels, roam
O'er wild and mountain, all the land their home:
— Thither he long'd to send that book, unseal'd,
Whose words are life, whose leaves his wounds had heal'd;
That Ishmael, living by his sword and bow,
Might thus again the God of Abraham know;
And Meccan Pilgrims to Caäba's shrine,
Like locusts marching in perpetual line,
Might quit the broad, to choose the narrow path,
That leads to glory, and reclaims from wrath.

Fired with the hope to bless his native soil,
Years roll'd unfelt, in consecrated toil,
To mould the truths which holy writers teach
In the loved accents of his mother's speech;
While, like the sun, that always to the west
Leads the bright day, his fervent spirit press'd,
Thither a purer light from heaven to dart,
— The only light that reaches to the heart;

Whose deserts blossom where its beams are shed,
The blind behold them, and they raise the dead.
Nor by Arabia were his labors bound,
To Persian lips he taught "the joyful sound."
Would he had held unchanged that high career!
— But Sabat fell like lightning from his sphere:
Once with the morning stars God's works he sung;
Anon a Serpent, with envenom'd tongue,
Like that apostate fiend who tempted Eve,
Gifted with speech, — he spake but to deceive.

Let pity o'er his errors cast a veil!
Haste to the sequel of his tragic tale.
Sabat became a vagabond on earth;
— He chose the Sinner's way, the Scorner's mirth;
Now feign'd contrition with obdurate tears,
Then wore a bravery that betray'd his fears;
With oaths and curses now his Lord denied,
And strangled guilty shame with desperate pride;
While inly-rack'd, he proved what culprits feel,
When conscience breaks remembrance on the wheel.
At length an outlaw through the orient isles,
Snared in the subtilty of his own wiles,
He perish'd in an unexpected hour,
To glut the vengeance of barbarian power;
With sackcloth shrouded, to a millstone bound,
And in the' abysses of the ocean drown'd.
— Oh! what a plunge into the dark was there!
How ended life? — In blasphemy or prayer?
The winds are fled that heard his parting cry,
The waves that stifled it make no reply.

When, at the resurrection of the Just,
Earth shall yield back Abdallah from the dust,
The sea, like rising clouds, give up its dead,
Then from the deep shall Sabat lift his head.
With waking millions round the judgment-seat,
Once, and but once again, those twain shall meet,
To part for ever, — or to part no more:
— But who the' eternal secret shall explore,
When Justice seals the gates of heaven and hell?
The rest — that day, that day alone, will tell.

1821.

THE ALPS:

A REVERIE.

PART I. *Day.*

THE mountains of this glorious land
Are conscious beings to mine eye,
When at the break of day they stand
Like giants, looking through the sky,
To hail the sun's unrisen car,
That gilds their diadems of snow;
While one by one, as star by star,
Their peaks in ether glow.

Their silent presence fills my soul,
When, to the horizontal ray,
The many-tinctured vapors roll
In evanescent wreaths away,
And leave them naked on the scene,
The emblems of eternity,
The same as they have ever been,
And shall for ever be.

Yet through the valley while I range,
Their cliffs, like images in dreams,
Color and shape, and station change;
Here crags and caverns, woods and streams,

And seas of adamantine ice,
With gardens, vineyards, fields embraced,
Open a way to Paradise,
Through all the splendid waste.

The goats are hanging on the rocks,
Wide through their pastures roam the herds;
Peace on the uplands feeds her flocks,
Till suddenly the king of birds
Pouncing a lamb, they start for fear;
He bears his bleating prize on high;
The well-known plaint his nestlings hear,
And raise a ravening cry.

The sun in morning freshness shines;
At noon behold his orb o'ercast;
Hollow and dreary o'er the pines,
Like distant ocean, moans the blast;
The mountains darken at the sound,
Put on their armor, and anon,
In panoply of clouds wrapt round,
Their forms from sight are gone.

Hark! war in heaven! — the battle-shout
Of thunder rends the echoing air;
Lo! war in heaven! — thick-flashing out
Through torrent-rains red lightnings glare,
As through the Alps, with mortal ire,
At once a thousand voices raised,
And with a thousand swords of fire
At once in conflict blazed.

Part II. *Night.*

Come, golden Evening, in the west
Enthrone the storm-dispelling sun,
And let the triple rainbow rest
O'er all the mountain-tops: — 'tis done;
The deluge ceases; bold and bright
The rainbow shoots from hill to hill;
Down sinks the sun; on presses night;
— Mont Blanc is lovely still.

There take thy stand, my spirit; — spread
The world of shadows at thy feet;
And mark how calmly, overhead,
The stars like saints in glory meet:
While hid in solitude sublime,
Methinks I muse on Nature's tomb,
And hear the passing foot of Time
Step through the gloom.

All in a moment, crash on crash,
From precipice to precipice,
An avalanche's ruins dash
Down to the nethermost abyss;
Invisible, the ear alone
Follows the uproar till it dies;
Echo on echo, groan for groan,
From deep to deep replies.

Silence again the darkness seals, —
Darkness that may be felt; — but soon
The silver-clouded east reveals
The midnight spectre of the moon;
In half-eclipse she lifts her horn,
Yet, o'er the host of heaven supreme,
Brings the faint semblance of a morn
With her awakening beam.

Ha! at her touch, these Alpine heights
Unreal mockeries appear;
With blacker shadows, ghastlier lights,
Enlarging as she climbs the sphere;
A crowd of apparitions pale!
I hold my breath in chill suspense,
— They seem so exquisitely frail, —
Lest they should vanish hence.

I breathe again, I freely breathe;
Lake of Geneva! thee I trace,
Like Dian's crescent far beneath,
And beautiful as Dian's face.
Pride of this land of liberty!
All that thy waves reflect I love;
Where heaven itself, brought down to thee,
Looks fairer than above.

Safe on thy banks again I stray,
The trance of poesy is o'er,
And I am here at dawn of day,
Gazing on mountains as before;

For all the strange mutations wrought
Were magic feats of my own mind;
Thus, in the fairy-land of thought,
Whate'er I seek I find.

Yet, O ye everlasting hills!
Buildings of God not made with hands,
Whose word performs whate'er He wills,
Whose word, though ye shall perish, stands;
Can there be eyes that look on you,
Till tears of rapture make them dim,
Nor in his works the Maker view,
Then lose his works in him?

By me, when I behold Him not,
Or love Him not when I behold,
Be all I ever knew forgot;
My pulse stand still, my heart grow cold;
Transform'd to ice, 'twixt earth and sky,
On yonder cliff my form be seen,
That all may ask, but none reply,
What my offence hath been.

1822.

QUESTIONS AND ANSWERS.

Flowers, wherefore do ye bloom?
— We strew thy pathway to the tomb.

Stars, wherefore do ye rise?
— To light thy spirit to the skies.

Fair Moon, why dost thou wane?
— That I may wax again.

O Sun, what makes thy beams so bright?
— The Word that said, — "Let there be light."

Planets, what guides you in your course?
— Unseen, unfelt, unfailing force.

Nature, whence sprang thy glorious frame?
— My Maker call'd me, and I came.

O Light, thy subtle essence who may know?
— Ask not; for all things but myself I show.

What is yon arch which everywhere I see?
— The sign of omnipresent Deity.

Where rests the horizon's all embracing zone?
— Where earth, God's footstool, touches heaven, his
throne.

Ye clouds, what bring ye in your train?
— God's embassies, — storm, lightning, hail, or rain.

Winds, whence and whither do ye blow?
— Thou must be born again to know.

Bow in the cloud, what token dost thou bear?
— That Justice still cries "*strike*," and Mercy "*spare*."

Dews of the morning, wherefore were ye given?
— To shine on earth, then rise to heaven.

Rise, glitter, break; yet, Bubble, tell me why?
— To show the course of all beneath the sky.

Stay, Meteor, stay thy falling fire!
— No, thus shall all the host of heaven expire.

Ocean, what law thy chainless waves confined?
— That which in Reason's limits holds thy mind.

Time, whither dost thou flee?
— I travel to Eternity.

Eternity, what art thou, — say?
— Time past, time present, time to come, — *to-day*.

Ye Dead, where can your dwelling be?
— The house for all the living: — come and see.

O Life, what is thy breath?
— A vapor lost in death.

O Death, how ends thy strife?
— In everlasting life.

O Grave, where is thy victory?
— Ask Him who rose again from me.

YOUTH RENEWED.

SPRING-FLOWERS, spring-birds, spring-breezes,
Are felt, and heard, and seen;
Light trembling transport seizes
My heart, — with sighs between;
These old enchantments fill the mind
With scenes and seasons far behind;
Childhood, its smiles and tears,
Youth, with its flush of years,
Its morning clouds and dewy prime,
More exquisitely touch'd by Time.

Fancies again are springing,
Like May-flowers in the vales;
While hopes, long lost, are singing,
From thorns, like nightingales;
And kindly spirits stir my blood,
Like vernal airs that curl the flood:
There falls to manhood's lot
A joy, which youth has not,
A dream more beautiful than truth,
— Returning Spring renewing Youth.

Thus sweetly to surrender
The present for the past;

In sprightly mood, yet tender,
Life's burden down to cast,
— This is to taste, from stage to stage,
Youth on the lees refined by age:
Like wine well kept and long,
Heady, nor harsh, nor strong,
With every annual cup, is quaff'd
A richer, purer, mellower draught.

Harrowgate, 1825.

THE BRIDAL AND THE BURIAL.

"Blessed is the bride whom the sun shines on;
Blessed is the corpse which the rain rains on."

I saw thee young and beautiful,
I saw thee rich and gay,
In the first blush of womanhood,
Upon thy wedding-day:
The church-bells rang,
And the little children sang, —
"Flowers, flowers, kiss her feet;
Sweets to the sweet;
The winter's past, the rains are gone;
Blessed is the bride whom the sun shines on."

I saw thee poor and desolate,
I saw thee fade away,
In broken-hearted widowhood,
Before thy locks were grey;
The death-bell rang,
And the little children sang, —
"Lilies, dress her winding-sheet;
Sweets to the sweet;
The summer's past, the sunshine gone;
Blessed is the corpse which the rain rains on."

"Blessed is the bride whom the sun shines on;
Blessed is the corpse which the rain rains on."

FRIENDS.

FRIEND after friend departs:
Who hath not lost a friend?
There is no union here of hearts,
That finds not here an end:
Were this frail world our only rest,
Living or dying, none were blest.

Beyond the flight of Time,
Beyond this vale of death,
There surely is some blessed clime,
Where life is not a breath,
Nor life's affections transient fire,
Whose sparks fly upward to expire.

There *is* a world above,
Where parting is unknown;
A whole eternity of love,
Form'd for the good alone;
And faith beholds the dying here
Translated to that happier sphere.

Thus star by star declines,
Till all are pass'd away,
As morning high and higher shines
To pure and perfect day;
Nor sink those stars in empty night,
— They hide themselves in heaven's own light.

1824.

A MOTHER'S LAMENT

ON THE DEATH OF HER INFANT DAUGHTER.

I LOVED thee, Daughter of my heart;
My Child, I loved thee dearly;
And though we only met to part,
— How sweetly! how severely! —
Nor life nor death can sever
My soul from thine for ever.

Thy days, my little one, were few,
An Angel's morning visit,
That came and vanish'd with the dew;
'T was here, 't is gone, where is it?
Yet didst thou leave behind thee
A clew for love to find thee.

The eye, the lip, the cheek, the brow,
The hands stretch'd forth in gladness,
All life, joy, rapture, beauty now,
Then dash'd with infant sadness,
Till, brightening by transition,
Return'd the fairy vision: —

Where are they now? — those smiles, those tears,
Thy Mother's darling treasure?

She sees them still, and still she hears
Thy tones of pain or pleasure,
To her quick pulse revealing
Unutterable feeling.

Hush'd in a moment on her breast,
Life, at the well-spring drinking,
Then cradled on her lap to rest,
In rosy slumber sinking,
Thy dreams — no thought can guess them;
And mine — no tongue express them.

For then this waking eye could see,
In many a vain vagary,
The things that never were to be,
Imaginations airy;
Fond hopes that mothers cherish,
Like still-born babes to perish.

Mine perish'd on thy early bier;
No — changed to forms more glorious,
They flourish in a higher sphere,
O'er time and death victorious;
Yet would these arms have chain'd thee,
And long from heaven detain'd thee.

Sarah! my last, my youngest love,
The crown of every other!
Though thou art born in heaven above,
I am thine only Mother.

Nor will affection let me
Believe thou canst forget me.

Then, — thou in heaven and I on earth, —
May this one hope delight us,
That thou wilt hail my second birth
When death shall re-unite us,
Where worlds no more can sever
Parent and child for ever.

THE WIDOW AND THE FATHERLESS.

Well, thou art gone, and I am left;
But, oh! how cold and dark to me
This world, of every charm bereft,
Where all was beautiful with thee!

Though I have seen thy form depart
For ever from my widow'd eye,
I hold thee in mine inmost heart;
There, there at least, thou canst not die.

Farewell on earth; Heaven claim'd its own;
Yet, when from me thy presence went,
I was exchanged for God alone:
Let dust and ashes learn content.

Ha! those small voices silver-sweet!
Fresh from the fields my babes appear;
They fill my arms, they clasp my feet;
—"Oh! could your father see us here!"

THE DAISY IN INDIA.

The simple history of these stanzas is the following. A friend of mine, a scientific botanist, residing near Sheffield, had sent a package of sundry kinds of British seeds to the learned and venerable Doctor WILLIAM CAREY, one of the first Baptist Missionaries to India, where they had established themselves in the small Danish settlement of Serampore, in the province of Bengal. Some of the seeds had been inclosed in a bag, containing a portion of their native earth. In March, 1821, a letter of acknowledgment was received by his correspondent from the Doctor, who was himself well skilled in botany, and had a garden rich in plants, both tropical and European. In this inclosure he was wont to spend an hour every morning, before he entered upon those labors and studies which have rendered his name illustrious both at home and abroad, as one of the most accomplished of oriental scholars, and a translator of the Holy Scriptures into many of the Hindoo languages. In the letter afore-mentioned, which was shown to me, the good man says, — "That I might be sure not to lose any part of your valuable present, I shook the bag over a patch of earth in a shady place: on visiting which a few days afterwards, I found springing up, to my inexpressible delight, a *bellis perennis* of our English pastures. I know not that I ever enjoyed, since leaving Europe, a simple pleasure so exquisite as the sight of this *English* Daisy afforded me; not having seen one for upwards of thirty years, and never expecting to see one again."

On the perusal of this passage, the following stanzas seemed to spring up almost spontaneously in my mind, as the "little English Flower" in the good Doctor's garden, whom I imagined to be thus addressing it on its sudden appearance. — With great care and attention he was able to perpetuate "the Daisy in India," as an *annual* only, raised by seed from season to season. It may be observed that, amidst the luxuriance of tropical vegetation, there are comparatively few *small* plants, like the multifarious progeny of our native Flora.

There is a beautiful coincidence between a fact and a fiction in this circumstance. Among the many natural and striking expedients by which the ingenious author of *Robinson Crusoe* contrives to supply his hero on the desolate island with necessaries and comforts of life, not indigenous, we are informed, that Crusoe one day, long after his shipwreck and residence there, perceived some delicate blades of vegetation peeping forth, after the rains, on a patch of ground near his dwelling-place. Not knowing what they were, he watched their growth from day to day, till he ascertained, to his "inexpressible delight," that they were plants of some kind of English corn. He then recollected having shaken out on that spot the dusty refuse of "a bag" which had been used to hold grain for the fowls on shipboard. "With great care and attention" he was enabled to preserve the precious stalks till the full corn ripened in the ear. He then reaped the first fruits of this spontaneous harvest, sowed them again, and, till his release from captivity there, ate bread in his lonely abode,

"Placed far amid the melancholy main."

THRICE welcome, little English flower!
My mother-country's white and red,
In rose or lily, till this hour,
Never to me such beauty spread:
Transplanted from thine island-bed,
A treasure in a grain of earth,
Strange as a spirit from the dead,
Thine embryo sprang to birth.

Thrice welcome, little English flower!
Whose tribes, beneath our natal skies,
Shut close their leaves while vapors lower;
But, when the sun's gay beams arise,
With unabash'd but modest eyes,
Follow his motion to the west,
Nor cease to gaze till daylight dies,
Then fold themselves to rest.

Thrice welcome, little English flower!
To this resplendent hemisphere,
Where Flora's giant offspring tower
In gorgeous liveries all the year:
Thou, only thou, art little here,
Like worth unfriended and unknown,

Yet to my British heart more dear
Than all the torrid zone.

Thrice welcome, little English flower!
Of early scenes beloved by me,
While happy in my father's bower,
Thou shalt the blithe memorial be;
The fairy sports of infancy,
Youth's golden age, and manhood's prime,
Home, country, kindred, friends, — with thee,
I find in this far clime.

Thrice welcome, little English flower!
I'll rear thee with a trembling hand:
Oh, for the April sun and shower,
The sweet May dew of that fair land,
Where Daisies, thick as star-light, stand
In every walk! — that here may shoot
Thy scions, and thy buds expand,
A hundred from one root.

Thrice welcome, little English flower!
To me the pledge of hope unseen:
When sorrow would my soul o'erpower,
For joys that were, or might have been,
I call to mind, how, fresh and green,
I saw thee waking from the dust;
Then turn to heaven with brow serene,
And place in God my trust.

1822.

THE DROUGHT.

WRITTEN IN THE SUMMER OF 1826.

Hosea ii. 21, 22.

WHAT strange, what fearful thing hath come to
pass?
The ground is iron, and the heavens are brass;
Man on the withering harvests casts his eye,
"Give me your fruits in season, or I die;"
The timely Fruits implore their parent Earth,
"Where is thy strength to bring us forth to birth?"
The Earth, all prostrate, to the Clouds complains,
"Send to my heart your fertilizing rains;"
The Clouds invoke the Heavens,—"Collect, dispense
Through us your quickening, healing influence;"
The Heavens to Him that made them raise their
moan,
"Command thy blessing, and it shall be done:"
The Lord is in his temple:—hush'd and still,
The suppliant Universe awaits his will.

He speaks; and to the Clouds the Heavens dis-
pense,
With lightning-speed, their genial influence;

The gathering, breaking Clouds pour down their rains,
Earth drinks the bliss through all her eager veins;
From teeming furrows start the Fruits to birth,
And shake their treasures on the lap of Earth;
Man sees the harvest grow beneath his eye,
Turns, and looks up with rapture to the sky;
All that have breath and being now rejoice;
All Nature's voices blend in one great voice,
"Glory to God, who thus himself makes known!"
— When shall all tongues confess Him God alone?

Lord! as the rain comes down from Heaven, — the rain
Which waters Earth, nor thence returns in vain,
But makes the tree to bud, the grass to spring,
And feeds and gladdens every living thing, —
So may thy word, upon a world destroy'd,
Come down in blessing, and return not void;
So may it come in universal showers,
And fill Earth's dreariest wilderness with flowers,
— With flowers of promise fill the world, within
Man's heart, laid waste and desolate by sin;
Where thorns and thistles curse the infested ground,
Let the rich fruits of righteousness abound;
And trees of life, for ever fresh and green,
Flourish where trees of death alone have been;
Let Truth look down from heaven, Hope soar above,
Justice and Mercy kiss, Faith work by Love;

Nations new-born their fathers' idols spurn;
The Ransom'd of the Lord with songs return;
Heralds the year of Jubilee proclaim;
Bow every knee at the Redeemer's name;
O'er lands, with darkness, thraldom, guilt, o'erspread,
In light, joy, freedom, be the Spirit shed;
Speak Thou the word: to Satan's power say, "Cease,"
But to a world of pardon'd sinners, "Peace."
—Thus in thy grace, LORD GOD, Thyself make known;
Then shall all tongues confess Thee GOD alone.

THE STRANGER AND HIS FRIEND.

"Ye have done it unto me." — *Matt.* xxv. 40.

A POOR wayfaring Man of grief
Hath often cross'd me on my way,
Who sued so humbly for relief,
That I could never answer "Nay:"
I had not power to ask his name,
Whither he went, or whence he came,
Yet was there something in his eye
That won my love, I knew not why.

Once, when my scanty meal was spread,
He enter'd; — not a word he spake; —
Just perishing for want of bread;
I gave him all; he bless'd it, brake,
And ate, — but gave me part again;
Mine was an Angel's portion then,
For while I fed with eager haste,
That crust was manna to my taste.

I spied him, where a fountain burst
Clear from the rock; his strength was gone;
The heedless water mock'd his thirst,
He heard it, saw it hurrying on:

I ran to raise the sufferer up;
Thrice from the stream he drain'd my cup,
Dipt, and return'd it running o'er;
I drank, and never thirsted more.

'T was night; the floods were out; it blew
A winter hurricane aloof;
I heard his voice abroad, and flew
To bid him welcome to my roof;
I warm'd, I clothed, I cheer'd my guest,
Laid him on my own couch to rest;
Then made the hearth my bed, and seem'd
In Eden's garden while I dream'd.

Stript, wounded, beaten, nigh to death,
I found him by the highway-side:
I roused his pulse, brought back his breath,
Revived his spirit, and supplied
Wine, oil, refreshment; he was heal'd;
— I had myself a wound conceal'd;
But from that hour forgot the smart,
And Peace bound up my broken heart.

In prison I saw him next, condemn'd
To meet a traitor's doom at morn;
The tide of lying tongues I stemm'd,
And honor'd him 'midst shame and scorn:
My friendship's utmost zeal to try,
He ask'd if I for him would die;
The flesh was weak, my blood ran chill,
But the free spirit cried, "I will."

Then in a moment to my view
The Stranger darted from disguise;
The tokens in his hands I knew,
My Saviour stood before mine eyes:
He spake; and my poor name He named;
"Of me thou hast not been ashamed:
These deeds shall thy memorial be;
Fear not, thou didst them unto Me."

Scarborough, December, 1826.

A SEA PIECE.

IN THREE SONNETS.

SCENE. — *Bridlington Quay*, 1824.

I.

AT nightfall, walking on the cliff-crown'd shore,
Where sea and sky were in each other lost;
Dark ships were scudding through the wild uproar,
Whose wrecks ere morn must strew the dreary coast;
I mark'd one well-moor'd vessel tempest-tost,
Sails reef'd, helm lash'd, a dreadful siege she bore,
Her deck by billow after billow cross'd,
While every moment she might be no more:
Yet firmly anchor'd on the nether sand,
Like a chain'd Lion ramping at his foes,
Forward and rearward still she plunged and rose,
Till broke her cable; — then she fled to land,
With all the waves in chase; throes following throes;
She 'scaped, — she struck, — she stood upon the strand.

II.

The morn was beautiful, the storm gone by;
Three days had pass'd; I saw the peaceful main,
One molten mirror, one illumined plane,
Clear as the blue, sublime, o'erarching sky:

On shore that lonely vessel caught mine eye,
Her bow was seaward, all equipt her train,
Yet to the sun she spread her wings in vain,
Like a caged Eagle, impotent to fly;
There fix'd as if for ever to abide;
Far down the beach had roll'd the low neap-tide,
Whose mingling murmur faintly lull'd the ear:
"Is this," methought, "is this the doom of pride,
Check'd in the onset of thy brave career,
Ingloriously to rot by piecemeal here?"

III.

Spring-tides return'd, and Fortune smiled; the bay
Received the rushing ocean to its breast;
While waves on waves innumerably prest,
Seem'd, with the prancing of their proud array,
Sea-horses, flash'd with foam, and snorting spray;
Their power and thunder broke that vessel's rest;
Slowly, with new expanding life possest,
To her own element she glid away;
Buoyant and bounding like the polar Whale,
That takes his pastime; every joyful sail
Was to the freedom of the wind unfurl'd,
While right and left the parted surges curl'd:
— Go, gallant Bark, with such a tide and gale,
I'll pledge thee to a voyage round the world.

ROBERT BURNS.

WHAT bird, in beauty, flight, or song,
Can with the Bard compare,
Who sang as sweet, and soar'd as strong,
As ever child of air?

His plume, his note, his form, could BURNS
For whim or pleasure change;
He was not one, but all by turns,
With transmigration strange.

The Blackbird, oracle of spring,
When flow'd his moral lay;
The Swallow wheeling on the wing,
Capriciously at play:

The Humming-bird, from bloom to bloom,
Inhaling heavenly balm;
The Raven, in the tempest's gloom;
The Halcyon, in the calm:

In "auld Kirk Alloway," the Owl,
At witching time of night;
By "bonnie Doon," the earliest Fowl
That caroll'd to the light.

He was the Wren amidst the grove,
When in his homely vein;
At Bannockburn the Bird of Jove,
With thunder in his train:

The Woodlark, in his mournful hours;
The Goldfinch, in his mirth;
The Thrush, a spendthrift of his powers,
Enrapturing heaven and earth;

The Swan, in majesty and grace,
Contemplative and still;
But roused, — no Falcon, in the chase,
Could like his satire kill.

The Linnet in simplicity,
In tenderness the Dove;
But more than all beside was he
The Nightingale in love.

Oh! had he never stoop'd to shame,
Nor lent a charm to vice,
How had Devotion loved to name
That Bird of Paradise!

Peace to the dead! — In Scotia's choir
Of Minstrels great and small,
He sprang from his spontaneous fire,
The Phœnix of them all.

1820.

A THEME FOR A POET.

1814.

Written in contemplation of a Poem on the Evangelization of one of the most degraded tribes of heathens. This the Author some years afterwards attempted, and partly executed, in "GREENLAND," in five cantos, of which the following were the opening lines, but withdrawn, as inapplicable to the unfinished work, when it was published.

Give me a theme to grace an Angel's tongue,
A theme to which a lyre was never strung;
Barbarian hordes, by Satan's craft enthrall'd,
From chains to freedom, guilt to glory call'd;
The deeds of men unfriended and unknown,
Sent forth by Him who loves and saves his own,
With faithful toil a barren land to bless,
And feed his flocks amid the wilderness.

These lines were afterwards adopted as a motto to the second volume of the last edition of Crantz's Greenland, including the history of the Missions of the Moravian Brethren there, which was begun in the year 1733. (See also the notes to "GREENLAND," the leading Poem in this Volume.)

THE arrow that shall lay me low,
Was shot from Death's unerring bow,
The moment of my breath;
And every footstep I proceed,
It tracks me with increasing speed;
I turn, — it meets me, — Death
Has given such impulse to that dart,
It points for ever at my heart.

And soon of me it must be said,
That I have lived, that I am dead;
Of all I leave behind,
A few may weep a little while,
Then bless my memory with a smile:
What monument of mind
Shall I bequeathe to deathless Fame,
That after-times may love my name?

Let Southey sing of war's alarms,
The pride of battle, din of arms,
The glory and the guilt, —
Of nations barb'rously enslaved,
Of realms by patriot valor saved,
Of blood insanely spilt,
And millions sacrificed to fate,
To make one little mortal great.

Let Scott, in wilder strains, delight
To chant the Lady and the Knight,
The tournament, the chase,
The wizard's deed without a name,
Perils by ambush, flood, and flame;
Or picturesquely trace
The hills that form a world on high,
The lake that seems a downward sky.

Let Byron, with untrembling hand,
Impetuous foot and fiery brand,
Lit at the flames of hell,
Go down and search the human heart,

Till fiends from every corner start,
Their crimes and plagues to tell:
Then let him fling the torch away,
And sun his soul in heaven's pure day.

Let Wordsworth weave, in mystic rhyme,
Feelings ineffably sublime,
And sympathies unknown;
Yet so our yielding breasts enthrall,
His Genius shall possess us all,
His thoughts become our own,
And, strangely pleased, we start to find
Such hidden treasures in *our* mind.

Let Campbell's sweeter numbers flow
Through every change of joy and woe;
Hope's morning dreams display,
The Pennsylvanian cottage wild,
The frenzy of O'Connor's child,
Or Linden's dreadful day;
And still in each new form appear
To every Muse and Grace more dear.

Transcendent Masters of the lyre!
Not to your honors I aspire;
Humbler yet higher views
Have touch'd my spirit into flame:
The pomp of fiction I disclaim;
Fair Truth! be thou my muse;
Reveal in splendor deeds obscure,
Abase the proud, exalt the poor.

I sing the men who left their home,
Amidst barbarian hordes to roam,
Who land and ocean cross'd,
Led by a load-star, mark'd on high
By Faith's unseen, all-seeing eye, —
To seek and save the lost;
Where'er the curse on Adam spread,
To call his offspring from the dead.

Strong in the great Redeemer's name,
They bore the cross, despised the shame;
And, like their Master here,
Wrestled with danger, pain, distress,
Hunger, and cold, and nakedness,
And every form of fear;
To feel his love their only joy,
To tell that love their sole employ.

O Thou, who wast in Bethlehem born,
The Man of sorrows and of scorn,
Jesus, the sinner's Friend!
— O Thou, enthroned in filial right,
Above all creature-power and might;
Whose kingdom shall extend,
Till earth, like heaven, thy name shall fill,
And men, like angels, do thy will: —

Thou, whom I love, but cannot see,
My Lord, my God! look down on me;
My low affections raise;
The spirit of liberty impart;

Enlarge my soul, inflame my heart,
And, while I spread thy praise,
Shine on my path, in mercy shine,
Prosper my work, and make it thine.

1818.

NIGHT.

Night is the time for rest;
How sweet, when labors close,
To gather round an aching breast
The curtain of repose,
Stretch the tired limbs, and lay the head
Down on our own delightful bed!

Night is the time for dreams;
The gay romance of life,
When truth that is, and truth that seems,
Mix in fantastic strife:
Ah! visions, less beguiling far
Than waking dreams by daylight are!

Night is the time for toil;
To plough the classic field,
Intent to find the buried spoil
Its wealthy furrows yield;
Till all is ours that sages taught,
That poets sang, and heroes wrought.

Night is the time to weep;
To wet with unseen tears
Those graves of memory, where sleep
The joys of other years;

Hopes, that were Angels at their birth,
But died when young like things of earth.

Night is the time to watch;
O'er ocean's dark expanse,
To hail the Pleiades, or catch
The full moon's earliest glance,
That brings into the home-sick mind
All we have loved and left behind.

Night is the time for care;
Brooding on hours misspent,
To see the spectre of Despair
Come to our lonely tent;
Like Brutus, 'midst his slumbering host,
Summon'd to die by Cæsar's ghost.

Night is the time to think;
When, from the eye, the soul
Takes flight, and, on the utmost brink
Of yonder starry pole,
Discerns beyond the abyss of night
The dawn of uncreated light.

Night is the time to pray;
Our Saviour oft withdrew
To desert mountains far away;
So will his followers do,
Steal from the throng to haunts untrod,
And commune there alone with God.

Night is the time for Death;
When all around is peace,
Calmly to yield the weary breath,
From sin and suffering cease,
Think of heaven's bliss, and give the sign
To parting friends; — such death be mine!

Harrowgate, September, 1821.

MEET AGAIN!*

JOYFUL words, — we meet again!
Love's own language, comfort darting
Through the souls of friends at parting:
Life in death, we meet again!

While we walk this vale of tears,
Compass'd round with care and sorrow,
Gloom to-day, and storm to-morrow,
"Meet again!" our bosom cheers.

Far in exile, when we roam,
O'er our lost endearments weeping,
Lonely, silent vigils keeping,
"Meet again!" transports us home.

When this weary world is past,
Happy they, whose spirits soaring,
Vast eternity exploring,
"Meet again" in heaven at last.

* The seven following pieces were written for "Select Foreign Airs," published some time ago under the title of "Polyhymnia," which accounts for the peculiar rhythm adopted in several of them. The first were paraphrased from the German; the words of the remaining three are original.

VIA CRUCIS, VIA LUCIS.

NIGHT turns to day:—
When sullen darkness lowers,
And heaven and earth are hid from sight,
Cheer up, cheer up;
Ere long the opening flowers,
With dewy eyes, shall shine in light.

Storms die in calms:—
When over land and ocean
Roll the loud chariots of the wind,
Cheer up, cheer up;
The voice of wild commotion
Proclaims tranquillity behind.

Winter wakes spring:—
When icy blasts are blowing
O'er frozen lakes, through naked trees,
Cheer up, cheer up;
All beautiful and glowing,
May floats in fragrance on the breeze.

War ends in peace:—
Though dread artillery rattle,
And ghastly corses load the ground,
Cheer up, cheer up;

Where groan'd the field of battle,
The song, the dance, the feast go round.

Toil brings repose: —
With noontide fervors beating,
When droop thy temples o'er thy breast,
Cheer up, cheer up;
Grey twilight, cool and fleeting,
Wafts on its wing the hour of rest.

Death springs to life: —
Though brief and sad thy story,
Thy years all spent in care and gloom,
Look up, look up;
Eternity and glory
Dawn through the portals of the tomb.

THE PILGRIM.

How blest the Pilgrim, who in trouble
Can lean upon a bosom-friend;
Strength, courage, hope with him redouble,
When foes assail, or griefs impend;
Care flees before his footsteps, straying,
At daybreak, o'er the purple heath;
He plucks the wild flowers round him playing,
And binds their beauty in a wreath.

More dear to him the fields and mountains,
When with his friend abroad he roves,
Rests in the shade near sunny fountains,
Or talks by moonlight through the groves:
For him the vine expands its clusters,
Spring wakes for him her woodland quire;
Yea, when the storm of winter blusters,
'T is summer round his evening fire.

In good old age serenely dying,
When all he loved forsakes his view,
Sweet is affection's voice replying,
"I follow soon," to his "Adieu!"
Even then, though earthly ties are riven,
The spirit's union will not end;
— Happy the man, whom Heaven hath given,
In life and death, a faithful friend.

GERMAN WAR SONG.*

HEAVEN speed the righteous sword,
And freedom be the word!
Come, brethren, hand in hand,
Fight for your father-land!

Germania from afar
Invokes her sons to war;
Awake! put forth your powers,
And victory must be ours.

On to the combat, on!
Go where your sires have gone:
Their might unspent remains,
Their pulse is in our veins.

On to the battle, on!
Rest will be sweet anon;
The slave may yield, may fly,
We conquer, or we die!

* The simple and sublime original of these stanzas, with the fine air by Hümmel, became the national song of Germany, and was sung by the soldiers especially, during the latter campaigns of the war, when Bonaparte was twice dethroned, and Europe finally delivered from French predominance.

O Liberty! thy form
Shines through the battle-storm;
Away with fear, away,
Let justice win the day.

REMINISCENCES.

Where are ye with whom in life I started,
Dear companions of my golden days?
Ye are dead, estranged from me, or parted,
— Flown, like morning clouds, a thousand ways.

Where art thou, in youth my friend and brother,
Yea, in soul my friend and brother still?
Heaven received thee, and on earth none other
Can the void in my lorn bosom fill.

Where is she, whose looks were love and gladness?
— Love and gladness I no longer see!
She is gone; and, since that hour of sadness,
Nature seems her sepulchre to me.

Where am I? — life's current faintly flowing
Brings the welcome warning of release;
Struck with death, ah! whither am I going?
All is well, — my spirit parts in peace.

THE AGES OF MAN.

Youth, fond youth! to thee, in life's gay morning,
New and wonderful are heaven and earth;
Health the hills, content the fields adorning,
Nature rings with melody and mirth;
Love invisible, beneath, above,
Conquers all things; all things yield to love.

Time, swift time, from years their motion stealing,
Unperceived hath sober manhood brought;
Truth, her pure and humble forms revealing,
Peoples fancy's fairy-land with thought;
Then the heart, no longer prone to roam,
Loves, loves best, the quiet bliss of home.

Age, old age, in sickness, pain, and sorrow,
Creeps with lengthening shadow o'er the scene;
Life was yesterday, 't is death to-morrow,
And to-day the agony between:
Then how longs the weary soul for thee,
Bright and beautiful eternity!

ASPIRATIONS OF YOUTH.

HIGHER, higher will we climb
Up the mount of glory,
That our names may live through time
In our country's story;
Happy, when her welfare calls,
He who conquers, he who falls.

Deeper, deeper let us toil
In the mines of knowledge;
Nature's wealth and learning's spoil
Win from school and college;
Delve we there for richer gems
Than the stars of diadems.

Onward, onward will we press
Through the path of duty;
Virtue is true happiness,
Excellence true beauty;
Minds are of supernal birth,
Let us make a heaven of earth.

Close and closer then we knit
Hearts and hands together,
Where our fire-side comforts sit
In the wildest weather;

Oh! they wander wide, who roam,
For the joys of life, from home.

Nearer, dearer bands of love
Draw our souls in union,
To our Father's house above,
To the saints' communion;
Thither every hope ascend,
There may all our labors end.

A HERMITAGE.

WHOSE is this humble dwelling-place,
The flat turf-roof with flowers o'ergrown?
Ah! here the tenant's name I trace,
Moss-cover'd, on the threshold stone.

Well, he has peace within and rest,
Though nought of all the world beside;
Yet, stranger, deem not him unblest,
Who knows not avarice, lust, or pride.

Nothing he asks, nothing he cares
For all that tempts or troubles round;
He craves no feast, no finery wears,
Nor once o'ersteps his narrow bound.

No need of light, though all be gloom,
To cheer his eye, — that eye is blind;
No need of fire in this small room,
He recks not tempest, rain, or wind.

No gay companion here; no wife
To gladden home with true-love smiles;
No children, — from the woes of life
To win him with their artless wiles.

Nor joy, nor sorrow, enter here,
Nor throbbing heart, nor aching limb;
No sun, no moon, no stars appear,
And man and brute are nought to him.

This dwelling is a hermit's cave,
With space alone for one poor bed;
This dwelling is a mortal's grave,
Its sole inhabitant is dead.

1822.

THE FALLING LEAF.

Were I a trembling leaf,
On yonder stately tree,
After a season gay and brief,
Condemn'd to fade and flee:

I should be loth to fall
Beside the common way,
Weltering in mire, and spurn'd by all,
Till trodden down to clay.

Nor would I choose to die
All on a bed of grass,
Where thousands of my kindred lie,
And idly rot in mass.

Nor would I like to spread
My thin and wither'd face
In *hortus siccus*, pale and dead,
A mummy of my race.

No, — on the wings of air
Might I be left to fly,
I know not and I heed not where,
A waif of earth and sky!

Or flung upon the stream,
Curl'd like a fairy-boat,
As through the changes of a dream,
To the world's end to float!

Who that hath ever been,
Could bear to be no more?
Yet who would tread again the scene,
He trod through life before?

On, with intense desire,
Man's spirit will move on;
It seems to die, yet, like heaven's fire,
It is not quench'd, but gone.

Matlock, 1822.

ON PLANTING A TULIP-ROOT.

HERE lies a bulb, the child of earth,
Buried alive beneath the clod,
Ere long to spring, by second birth,
A new and nobler work of God.

'Tis said that microscopic power
Might through its swaddling folds descry
The infant-image of the flower,
Too exquisite to meet the eye.

This, vernal suns and rains will swell,
Till from its dark abode it peep,
Like Venus rising from her shell,
Amidst the spring-tide of the deep.

Two shapely leaves will first unfold,
Then, on a smooth elastic stem,
The verdant bud shall turn to gold,
And open in a diadem.

Not one of Flora's brilliant race
A form more perfect can display ;
Art could not feign more simple grace,
Nor Nature take a line away.

Yet, rich as morn of many a hue,
When flushing clouds through darkness strike,
The tulip's petals shine in dew,
All beautiful, — but none alike.

Kings, on their bridal, might unrobe
To lay their glories at its foot;
And queens their sceptre, crown, and globe,
Exchange for blossom, stalk, and root.

Here could I stand and moralize;
Lady, I leave that part to thee;
Be thy next birth in Paradise,
Thy life to come eternity!

1824.

THE ADVENTURE OF A STAR.

ADDRESSED TO A YOUNG LADY.

A STAR would be a flower;
So down from heaven it came,
And in a honeysuckle bower
Lit up its little flame.
There on a bank, beneath the shade,
By sprays, and leaves, and blossoms made,
It overlook'd the garden-ground,
— A landscape stretching ten yards round;
O what a change of place
From gazing through the' eternity of space!

Gay plants on every side
Unclosed their lovely blooms,
And scatter'd far and wide
Their ravishing perfumes:
The butterfly, the bee,
And many an insect on the wing,
Full of the spirit of the spring,
Flew round and round in endless glee,
Alighting here, ascending there,
Ranging and revelling everywhere.

Now all the flowers were up and drest
In robes of rainbow-color'd light;

The pale primroses look'd their best,
Peonies blush'd with all their might;
Dutch tulips from their beds
Flaunted their stately heads;
Auriculas, like belles and beaux,
Glittering with birthnight splendor, rose;
And polyanthuses display'd
The brilliance of their gold brocade:
Here hyacinths of heavenly blue
Shook their rich tresses to the morn,
While rose-buds scarcely show'd their hue,
But coyly linger'd on the thorn,
Till their loved nightingale, who tarried long,
Should wake them into beauty with his song.
The violets were past their prime,
Yet their departing breath
Was sweeter, in the blast of death,
Than all the lavish fragrance of the time.

Amidst this gorgeous train,
Our truant star shone forth in vain;
Though in a wreath of periwinkle,
Through whose fine gloom it strove to twinkle,
It seem'd no bigger to the view
Than the light spangle in a drop of dew.
— Astronomers may shake their polls,
And tell me, — every orb that rolls
Through heaven's sublime expanse
Is sun or world, whose speed and size

Confound the stretch of mortal eyes,
In Nature's mystic dance:
It may be so
For aught I know,
Or aught indeed that they can show;
Yet till they prove what they aver,
From this plain truth I will not stir,
— A star's a star! — but when I think
Of sun or world, the star I sink;
Wherefore in verse, at least in mine,
Stars like themselves, in spite of fate, shall shine.

Now, to return (for we have wander'd far)
To what was nothing but a simple star;
— Where all was jollity around,
No fellowship the stranger found.
Those lowliest children of the earth,
That never leave their mother's lap,
Companions in their harmless mirth,
Were smiling, blushing, dancing there,
Feasting on dew, and light, and air,
And fearing no mishap,
Save from the hand of lady fair,
Who, on her wonted walk,
Pluck'd one and then another,
A sister or a brother,
From its elastic stalk;
Happy, no doubt, for one sharp pang, to die
On her sweet bosom, withering in her eye.

Thus all day long that star's hard lot,
While bliss and beauty ran to waste,
Was but to witness on the spot
Beauty and bliss it could not taste.
At length the sun went down, and then
Its faded glory came again;
With brighter, bolder, purer light,
It kindled through the deepening night,
Till the green bower, so dim by day,
Glow'd like a fairy-palace with its beams;
In vain, for sleep on all the borders lay,
The flowers were laughing in the land of dreams.
Our star, in melancholy state,
Still sigh'd to find itself alone,
Neglected, cold, and desolate,
Unknowing and unknown.
Lifting at last an anxious eye,
It saw that circlet empty in the sky
Where it was wont to roll
Within a hair-breadth of the pole:
In that same instant, sore amazed,
On the strange blank all Nature gazed;
Travellers, bewilder'd for their guide,
In glens and forests lost their way;
And ships, on ocean's trackless tide,
Went fearfully astray.
The star, now wiser for its folly, knew
Its duty, dignity, and bliss at home;
So up to heaven again it flew,
Resolved no more to roam.

One hint the humble bard may send
To her for whom these lines are penn'd:
— O may it be enough for her
To shine in her own character!
O may she be content to grace,
On earth, in heaven, her proper place!

1825.

INSCRIPTION

UNDER THE PICTURE OF AN AGED NEGRO-WOMAN.

Art thou a *woman?* — so am I; and all
That woman can be, I have been, or am;
A daughter, sister, consort, mother, widow.
Whiche'er of these *thou* art, O be the friend
Of one who is what thou canst never be!
Look on thyself, thy kindred, home, and country,
Then fall upon thy knees, and cry "Thank God,
An English woman cannot be a Slave!"

Art thou a *man?* — Oh! I have known, have loved,
And lost, all that to woman man can be;
A father, brother, husband, son, who shared
My bliss in freedom, and my woe in bondage.
— A childless widow now, a friendless slave,
What shall I ask of thee, since I have nought
To lose but life's sad burden; nought to gain
But heaven's repose? — these are beyond thy power;
Me thou canst neither wrong nor help; — what then?
Go to the bosom of thy family,
Gather thy little children round thy knees,
Gaze on their innocence; their clear, full eyes,

All fix'd on thine; and in their mother, mark
The loveliest look that woman's face can wear,
Her look of love, beholding them and thee:
Then, at the altar of your household joys,
Vow one by one, vow altogether, vow
With heart and voice, eternal enmity
Against oppression by your brethren's hands;
Till man nor woman under Britain's laws,
Nor son nor daughter born within her empire,
Shall buy, or sell, or hold, or be a slave.

Scarborough, December, 1826.

THOUGHTS AND IMAGES.

"Come like shadows, so depart." *Macbeth.*

The Diamond, in its native bed,
Hid like a buried star may lie,
Where foot of man must never tread,
Seen only by its Maker's eye:
And though imbuëd with beams to grace
His fairest work in woman's face,
Darkling, its fire may fill the void,
Where fix'd at first in solid night;
Nor, till the world shall be destroy'd,
Sparkle one moment into light.

The Plant, upspringing from the seed,
Expands into a perfect flower;
The virgin-daughter of the mead,
Wooed by the sun, the wind, the shower:
In loveliness beyond compare,
It toils not, spins not, knows no care;
Train'd by the secret hand, that brings
All beauty out of waste and rude,
It blooms its season, dies, and flings
Its germs abroad in solitude.

Almighty skill, in ocean's caves,
Lends the light Nautilus a form

To tilt along the Atlantic waves,
Fearless of rock, or shoal, or storm;
But, should a breath of danger sound,
With sails, quick-furl'd it dives profound,
And far beneath the tempest's path,
In coral grots, defies the foe,
That never brake, in heaviest wrath,
The sabbath of the deep below.

Up from his dream, on twinkling wings,
The Sky-lark soars amid the dawn;
Yet, while in Paradise he sings,
Looks down upon the quiet lawn,
Where flutters, in his little nest,
More love than music e'er express'd;
Then, though the Nightingale may thrill
The soul with keener ecstasy,
The merry bird of morn can fill
All Nature's bosom with his glee.

The Elephant, embower'd in woods,
Coeval with their trees might seem,
As though he drank from Indian floods
Life in a renovating stream:
Ages o'er him have come and fled;
Midst generations of the dead,
His bulk survives to feed and range,
Where ranged and fed of old his sires;
Nor knows advancement, lapse, or change,
Beyond their walks, till he expires.

Gem, flower, and fish, the bird, the brute,
Of every kind occult or known
(Each exquisitely form'd to suit
Its humble lot, and that alone),
Through ocean, earth, and air fulfil,
Unconsciously, their Maker's will,
Who gave, without their toil or thought,
Strength, beauty, instinct, courage, speed;
While through the whole his pleasure wrought
Whate'er his wisdom had decreed.

But Man, the masterpiece of God,
Man, in his Maker's image framed, —
Though kindred to the valley's clod,
Lord of this low creation named, —
In naked helplessness appears,
Child of a thousand griefs and fears:
To labor, pain, and trouble born,
Weapon, nor wing, nor sleight hath he;
Yet, like the sun, he brings his morn,
And is a king from infancy.

For, him no destiny hath bound
To do what others did before,
Pace the same dull perennial round,
And be a man, and be no more:
A man? — a self-will'd piece of earth,
Just as the lion is, by birth;
To hunt his prey, to wake, to sleep,
His father's joys and sorrows share,

His niche in Nature's temple keep,
And leave his likeness in his heir! —

No; infinite the shades between
The motley millions of our race;
No two, the changing moon hath seen
Alike in purpose, or in face;
Yet all aspire beyond their fate;
The least, the meanest, would be great;
The mighty future fills the mind,
That pants for more than earth can give:
Man, to this narrow sphere confined,
Dies when he but begins to live.

Oh! if there be no world on high
To yield his powers unfetter'd scope;
If man be only born to die,
Whence this inheritance of hope?
Wherefore to him alone were lent
Riches that never can be spent?
Enough, not more, to all the rest,
For life and happiness, was given;
To man, mysteriously unblest,
Too much for any state but heaven.

It is not thus; — it cannot be,
That one so gloriously endow'd
With views that reach eternity,
Should shine and vanish like a cloud:
Is there a God? — all Nature shows
There *is*, — and yet no *mortal* knows:

The mind that could this truth conceive,
Which brute sensation never taught,
No longer to the dust would cleave,
But grow immortal with the thought.

1819.

NARRATIVES.

NARRATIVES.

FAREWELL TO WAR;

BEING A PROLOGUE TO "LORD FALKLAND'S DREAM," AND "ARNOLD DE WINKELRIED, OR THE PATRIOT'S PASS-WORD."

PEACE to the trumpet! — no more shall my breath
Sound an alarm in the dull ear of death,
Nor startle to life from the truce of the tomb
The relics of heroes, to combat till doom.
Let Marathon sleep to the sound of the sea,
Let Hannibal's spectre haunt Cannæ for me;
Let Cressy and Agincourt tremble with corn,
And Waterloo blush with the beauty of morn;
I turn not the furrow for helmets and shields,
Nor sow dragon's teeth in their old fallow fields;
I will not, as bards have been wont, since the flood,
With the river of song swell the river of blood,
— The blood of the valiant, that fell in all climes,
— The song of the gifted, that hallow'd all crimes,
— All crimes in the war-fiend incarnate in one;
War, withering the earth — war, eclipsing the sun,

Despoiling, destroying, since discord began,
God's works and God's mercies, — man's labors and
man.

Yet war have I loved, and of war have I sung,
With my heart in my hand and my soul on my
tongue;
With all the affections that render life dear,
With the throbbings of hope and the flutterings of
fear,
— Of hope, that the sword of the brave might pre-
vail,
— Of fear, lest the arm of the righteous should fail.

But what was the war that extorted my praise?
What battles were fought in my chivalrous lays?
— The war against darkness contending with light;
The war against violence trampling down right;
— The battles of patriots, with banner unfurl'd,
To guard a child's cradle against an arm'd world;
Of peasants that peopled their ancestors' graves,
Lest their ancestors' homes should be peopled by
slaves.
I served, too, in wars and campaigns of the mind;
My pen was the sword, which I drew for mankind;
— In war against tyranny throned in the West,
— Campaigns to enfranchise the negro oppress'd;
In war *against* war, on whatever pretence,
For glory, dominion, revenge, or defence,

While murder and perfidy, rapine and lust,
Laid provinces desolate, cities in dust.

Yes, war *against* war was ever my pride;
My youth and my manhood in waging it died,
And age, with its weakness, its wounds, and its scars,
Still finds my free spirit unquench'd as the stars,
And he who would bend it to war must first bind
The waves of the ocean, the wings of the wind;
For I call it not war, which war's counsels o'erthrows,
I call it not war which gives nations repose;
'Tis judgment brought down on themselves by the proud,
Like lightning, by fools, from an innocent cloud.

I war against *all* war; — nor, till my pulse cease,
Will I throw down my weapons, because I love peace,
Because I love liberty, execrate strife,
And dread, most of *all* deaths, that slow death call'd life,
Dragg'd on by a vassal, in purple or chains,
The breath of whose nostrils, the blood in whose veins,
He calls not his own, nor holds from his God,
While it hangs on a king's or a sycophant's nod.

Around the mute trumpet, — no longer to breathe
War-clangors, my latest war-chaplets I wreathe,

Then hang them aloof on the time-stricken oak,
And thus in its shadow, heaven's blessing invoke: —
"Lord God! since the African's bondage is o'er,
And war in our borders is heard of no more,
May never, while Britain adores Thee, again
The malice of fiends or the madness of men,
Break the peace of our land, and by villainous wrong
Find a field for a hero, a hero for song."

1834.

LORD FALKLAND'S DREAM.

A. D. 1643.

"Io vo gridando, Pace! pace! pace!"

PETRARCA, *Canzone agli principi d'Italia, Esortazione alla Pace, A. D.* 1344.*

"In this unhappy battle (of Newbury) was slain the Lord Viscount Falkland, a person of such prodigious parts of learning and knowledge, of that inimitable sweetness and delight of conversation, of so flowing and obliging a humanity and goodness to mankind, and of that primitive simplicity and integrity of life, that if there were no other brand upon this odious and accursed war, than that single loss, it must be most infamous and execrable to all posterity.

'Turpe mori, post te, solo non posse dolore.'"

* * * * *

"From the entrance into that unnatural war, his natural cheerfulness and vivacity grew clouded; and a kind of sadness and dejection stole upon him, which he had never been used to. * * * After the King's return to Oxford, and the furious resolution of the two Houses not to admit any treaty for peace, those indispositions which had before touched him grew into a perfect habit of uncheerfulness; and he who had been so exactly easy and affable to all men, that his face and countenance was always present, and vacant to his company, and held any cloudiness or less pleasantness of the visage a kind of rudeness or incivility, became on a sudden less communicable, and thence very sad, pale, and exceedingly affected with the spleen. In his clothes and habit, which he minded before with more neatness, and industry, and expense, than is usual to so great a soul, he was not only incurious, but too negligent; and in his reception of suitors, and the necessary and casual addresses to his place (being Secretary of State to King Charles,) so

* "I go exclaiming Peace! peace! peace!" — From PETRARCH'S *Canzone to the Princes of Italy*, entitled "*An Exhortation to Peace.*"

quick, and sharp, and severe, that there wanted not some men (strangers to his nature and disposition) who believed him proud and imperious, from which no mortal man was ever more free."

* * * * *

"When there was any overture or hope of peace he would be more erect and vigorous, and exceedingly solicitous to press any thing which he thought might promote it; and, sitting among his friends, often, after a deep silence, and frequent sighs, would, with a shrill and sad accent, ingeminate the word '*Peace! peace!*' and would profess that the very agony of the war and view of the calamities and desolation the kingdom did and must endure, took his sleep from him, and would shortly break his heart."

CLARENDON'S *History*, vol. ii. part i.

WAR, civil war, was raging like a flood,
England lay weltering in her children's blood;
Brother with brother waged unnatural strife,
Sever'd were all the charities of life:
Two passions, — virtues they assumed to be, —
Virtues they *were*, — romantic loyalty,
And stern, unyielding patriotism, possess'd
Divided empire in the nation's breast;
As though two hearts might in one body reign,
And urge conflicting streams from vein to vein.
On either side the noblest spirits fought,
And highest deeds on either side were wrought:
Hampden in battle yesterday hath bled,
Falkland to-morrow joins the immortal dead;
The one for freedom perish'd — not in vain;
The other falls — a courtier without stain.

'T was on the eve of Newbury's doubtful fight;
O'er marshall'd foes came down the peace of night,
— Peace which, to eyes in living slumber seal'd,
The mysteries of the night to come reveal'd,

When that throng'd plain, now warm with heaving breath,
Should lie in cold, fix'd apathy of death.
Falkland from court and camp had glid away, [stray,
With Chaucer's shade,* through Speenham woods to
And pour in solitude, without control,
Through the dun gloom, the anguish of his soul.
— Falkland, the plume of England's chivalry,
The just, the brave, the generous, and the free!
— Nay, task not poetry to tell his praise,
Twine but a wreath of transitory bays,
To crown him, as he lives, from age to age,
In Clarendon's imperishable page;
Look there upon the very man, and see
What Falkland was, — what thou thyself shouldst be;
Patriot and loyalist, who veil'd to none,
He loved his country and his king in one,
And could no more, in his affections, part
That wedded pair, than pluck out half his heart:
Hence every wound that each the other gave,
Brought their best servant nearer to the grave.
Thither he hasten'd, withering in his prime,
The worm of sorrow wrought the work of time;
And England's woes had sunk him with their weight,
Had not the swifter sword foreclosed his date.

In sighs for her his spirit was exhaled,
He wept for her till power of weeping fail'd;

* The estate of Speenhamland, near Newbury, Burks, is said to have been the property and residence of Chaucer.

Pale, wasted, nerveless, absent, — he appear'd
To haunt the scenes which once his presence cheer'd;
As though some vampire from its cerements crept,
And drain'd health's fountain nightly while he slept;
But he slept *not;* — sleep from his eyelids fled,
All restless as the ocean's foam his bed;
The very agony of war, — the guilt
Of blood by kindred blood in hatred spilt,
Crush'd heart and hope; till foundering, tempest-
toss'd,
From gulfs to deeper gulfs, himself he lost.
Yet when he heard the drum to battle beat,
First at the onset, latest in retreat,
Eager to brave rebellion to the face,
Or hunt out peril in its hiding-place,
Falkland was slow to harm the' ignoble crowd,
He sought to raise the fall'n, strike down the proud,
Nor stood there one for parliament or throne
More choice of meaner lives, more reckless of his
own.

Oft from his lips a shrill, sad moan would start,
And cold misgivings creep around his heart,
When he beheld the plague of war increase,
And but one word found utterance — "Peace!
peace! peace!"

That eve he wander'd in his wayward mood,
Through thoughts more wildering than the maze of
wood,

Where, when the moon-beam flitted o'er his face,
He seem'd the' unquiet spectre of the place:
Rank thorns and briars, the rose and woodbine's
bloom
Perplex'd his path through checker'd light and
gloom;
Himself insensible of gloom or light,
Darkness within made all around him night;
Till the green beauty of a little glade,
That open'd up to heaven, his footsteps stay'd:
Eye, breath, and pulse, the sweet enchantment felt,
His heart with tenderness began to melt;
Trembling, he lean'd against a Druid oak,
Whose boughs bare token of the thunder-stroke,
With root unshaken, and with bole unbroke:
Then thus, while hope almost forgot despair,
Breathed his soul's burden on the tranquil air:—

"O, Britain! Britain! to thyself be true;
Land which the Roman never could subdue:
Oft though he pass'd thy sons beneath the yoke,
As oft thy sons the spears they bow'd to broke;
Others with home-wrought chains he proudly bound,
His own too weak to fetter thee he found;
Though garrison'd by legions, legions fail'd
To quell thy spirit,—thy spirit again prevail'd.
By him abandon'd, island-martyr! doom'd
To prove the fires of ages unconsumed,
Though Saxon, Dane, Norwegian, Gallic hordes,
In dire succession, gave thee laws and lords,

Conquer'd themselves by peace, — in every field,
The victor to the vanquish'd lost his shield.
To win my country, to usurp her throne,
Canute and William must forsake their own;
Invading rivers thus roll back the sea,
Then lose themselves in its immensity.

"But 't was thine own distractions lent them aid,
Enslaved by strangers, because self-betray'd;
Still self-distracted; — yet should foreign foe
Land *now*, another spirit thy sons would show;
King, nobles, parliament, and people, — all,
Like the Red Sea's returning waves, would feel,
And with one burst o'erwhelm the mightiest host.
— Would such a foe this hour were on thy coast!

"How oft, O Albion! since those twilight times,
Have wars intestine laid thee waste with crimes!
Tweed's borderers were hereditary foes,
Nor can one crown even now their feuds compose;
Thy peasantry were serfs to vassal lords,
Yoked with their oxen, tether'd to their swords:
Round their cross-banners kings thy bowmen ranged,
Till York and Lancaster their roses changed.
Those days, thank Heaven! those evil days, are past,
Yet wilt thou fall by suicide at last?
O England! England! from such frenzy cease,
And on thyself have mercy, — Peace! peace! peace!"

"Who talks of Peace? — sweet Peace is in her grave:
Save a lone widow, — from her offspring save!"

Exclaim'd a voice, scarce earthly, in his ear,
Withering his nerves with unaccustom'd fear;
His hand was on his sword, but ere he drew
The starting blade, a suppliant cross'd his view;
Forth from the forest rush'd a female form,
Like the moon's image hurrying through the storm;
Down in a moment at his feet, aghast,
Lock'd to his smiting knees, herself she cast.
Rent were her garments, and her hair unbound,
All fleck'd with blood from many an unstaunch'd wound,
Inflicted by the very hands that press'd,
In rose-lipp'd infancy, her yearning breast;
And ever and anon she look'd behind,
As though pursuing voices swell'd the wind;
Then shriek'd insanely, — "Peace is in her grave!
Save a lost mother, — from her children save!"
Wan with heart-sickness, ready to expire,
Her cheeks were ashes, but her eye was fire,
— Fire fix'd, as through the horror of the mine,
Sparks from the diamond's still water shine;
So where the cloud of death o'ershadowing hung,
Light in her eye from depth of darkness sprung,
Dazzling his sight, and kindling such a flame
Within his breast as nature could not name;
He knew her not; — that face he never saw;
He loved her not, — yet love, chastised by awe
And reverence, with mysterious terror mix'd,
His looks on hers in fascination fix'd.

"Who? — whence? — what wouldst thou?" Falkland cried at length:
His voice inspired her; up she rose in strength,
Gather'd her robe and spread her locks, to hide
The unsightly wounds; then fervently replied: —
"Behold a matron, widow'd and forlorn,
Yet many a noble son to me was born,
Flowers of my youth, and morning-stars of joy!
— They quarrell'd, fought, and slew my youngest boy;
Youngest and best beloved! — I rush'd between,
My darling from the fratricides to screen;
He perish'd; from my arms he dropp'd in death;
I felt him kiss my feet with his last breath;
The swords that smote him, flashing round my head,
Pierced me, — the murderers saw my blood, and fled, —
Their parent's blood; and she, unconscious why
She sought *thee* out, came here — came here to die.
'T is a strange tale; — 't is true, — and yet 't is not;
Follow me, Falkland, thou shalt see the spot, —
See my slain boy, — my life's own life, the pride
And hope of his poor mother, — but he died;
He died, — and *she* did *not;* — how can it be?
But I'm immortal! — Falkland, come and see."

She spake; while Falkland, more and more amazed,
On her ineffable demeanor gazed;
So vitally her form and features changed,
He thought his own clear senses were deranged;

Outraged and desolate she seem'd no more;
He follow'd; stately, she advanced before:
The thickets, at her touch, gave way, and made
A wake of moonlight through their deepest shade.
Anon he found himself on Newbury's plain,
Walking among the dying and the slain;
At every step in blood his foot was dyed,
He heard expiring groans on every side.
The battle-thunder had roll'd by; the smoke
Was vanish'd; calm and bright the morning broke,
While such estrangement o'er his mind was cast,
As though another day and night had past.
There, midst the nameless crowd, oft met his view
An eye, a countenance, which Falkland knew,
But knew not him; — that eye to ice congeal'd,
That countenance by death's blank signet seal'd:
Rebel and royalist alike laid low,
Where friend embraced not friend, but foe grasp'd foe;
Falkland had tears for each, and patriot sighs,
For both were Britons in that Briton's eyes.

Silent before him trod the lofty dame,
Breathlessly looking round her, till they came
Where shatter'd fences mark'd a narrow road:
Tracing that line, with prostrate corpses strow'd,
She turn'd their faces upward, one by one,
Till, suddenly, the newly-risen sun
Shot through the level air a ruddy glow,
That fell upon a visage white as snow;
Then with a groan of agony, so wild,
As if the soul within her spake, — "My child!

My child!" she said, and pointing, shrinking back,
Made way for Falkland. — Prone along the track
(A sight at once that warm'd and thrill'd with awe)
The perfect image of himself he saw,
Shape, feature, limb, the arms, the dress he wore,
And one wide, honorable wound before.
Then flash'd the fire of pride from Falkland's eye,
" 'T is glorious for our country thus to die;
'T is sweet to leave an everlasting name,
A heritage of clear and virtuous fame."
While thoughts like these his maddening brain possess'd,
And lightning pulses thunder'd through his breast;
While Falkland living stood o'er Falkland dead,
Fresh at his feet the corse's death-wound bled,
The eye met his with inexpressive glance,
Like the sleep-walker's in benumbing trance,
And o'er the countenance of rigid clay,
The flush of life came quick, then pass'd away;
A momentary pang convulsed the chest,
As though the heart, awaking from unrest,
Broke with the effort; — all again was still;
Chill through his tingling veins the blood ran, chill.
"Can this," he sigh'd, "be virtuous fame and clear?
Ah! what a field of fratricide is here!
Perish who may, — 't is England, England falls;
Triumph who will, — his vanquish'd country calls,
As I have done, — as I will never cease,
While I have breath and being — Peace! peace! peace!"

Here stoop'd the matron o'er the dead man's
face,
Kiss'd the cold lips, then caught in her embrace
The living Falkland; — as he turn'd to speak,
He felt his mother's tears upon his cheek:
He knew her, own'd her, and at once forgot
All but her earliest love, and his first lot.
Her looks, her tones, her sweet caresses, then
Brought infancy and fairy land again,
— Youth in the morn and maidenhood of life,
Ere fortune curst his father's house with strife,
And in an age when nature's laws were changed,
Mother and son, as heaven from earth, estranged.*

"Oh, Falkland! Falkland!" when her voice
found speech,
The lady cried; then took a hand of each,
And joining clasp'd them in her own, — "My son!
Behold thyself, for thou and he are one."
The dead man's hand grasp'd Falkland's with such
force,
He fell transform'd into that very corse,
As though the wound which slew his counterpart
That moment sent the death-shot through his heart.

When from that ecstasy he oped his eyes,
He thought his soul translated to the skies;

* There had been unhappy divisions in the family, both with respect to an inheritance which Falkland held from his grandfather, and the religion of his mother, who was a Roman Catholic.

The battle-field had disappear'd; the scene
Had changed to beauty, silent and serene;
City nor country look'd as heretofore;
A hundred years and half a hundred more
Had travell'd o'er him while entranced he lay;
England appear'd as England at *this* day,
In arts, arms, commerce, enterprise, and power,
Beyond the dreams of his devoutest hour,
When, with prophetic call, the patriot brought
Ages to come before creative thought.

With doubt, fear, joy, he look'd above, beneath,
Felt his own pulse, inhaled, and tried to breathe;
Next raised an arm, advanced a foot, then broke
Silence, yet only in a whisper spoke:
"My mother! are we risen from the tomb?
Is this the morning of the day of doom?"
No answer came; his mother was not there,
But, tall and beautiful beyond compare,
One, who might well have been an angel's bride,
Were angels mortal, glitter'd at his side.
It seem'd some mighty wizard had unseal'd
The book of fate, and in that hour reveal'd
The object of a passion all his own,
— A lady unexistent, or unknown,
Whose saintly image, in his heart enshrined.
Was but an emanation of his mind,
The ideal form of glory, goodness, truth,
Embodied now in all the flush of youth,
Yet not too exquisite to look upon:
He kneel'd to kiss her hand, — the spell was gone.

Even while his brain the dear illusion cross'd,
Her form of soft humanity was lost.
—Then, nymph nor goddess, of poetic birth,
E'er graced Jove's heaven, or stept on classic earth,
Like her in majesty;—the stars came down
To wreathe her forehead with a fadeless crown;
The sky enrobed her with ethereal blue,
And girt with orient clouds of many a hue;
The sun, enamour'd of that loveliest sight,
So veil'd his face with her benigner light, [streams,
That woods and mountains, valleys, rocks, and
Were only visible in her pure beams.

While Falkland, pale and trembling with surprise,
Admired the change, her stature seem'd to rise,
Till from the ground, on which no shadow spread,
To the arch'd firmament she rear'd her head;
And in the' horizon's infinite expanse,
He saw the British islands at a glance,
With intervening and encircling seas,
O'er which, from every port, with every breeze,
Exulting ships were sailing to all realms,
Whence vessels came, with strangers at their helms,
On Albion's shores all climes rejoiced to meet,
And pour their native treasures at her feet.

Then Falkland, in that glorious dame, descried
Not a dead parent, nor a phantom bride,
But *her* who ruled his soul, in either part,
At once the spouse and mother of his heart,

— His country, thus personified, in grace
And grandeur unconceived, before his face.
Then spake a voice, as from the primal sphere,
Heard by his spirit rather than his ear: —

"Henceforth let civil war for ever cease;
Henceforth, my sons and daughters, dwell in peace;
Amidst the ocean-waves that never rest,
My lovely Isle, be thou the halcyon's nest;
Amidst the nations, evermore in arms,
Be thou a haven, safe from all alarms;
Alone immovable 'midst ruins stand,
The' unfailing hope of every failing land:
To thee for refuge kings enthroned repair;
Slaves flock to breathe the freedom of thine air.
Hither, from chains and yokes, let exiles bend
Their footsteps; here the friendless find a friend;
The country of mankind shall Britain be,
The home of peace, the whole world's sanctuary."

The pageant fled; 'twas but a dream: he woke,
And found himself beneath the Druid-oak,
Where first the phantom on his vigil broke.

Around him gleam'd the morn's reviving light;
But distant trumpets summon'd to the fight,
And Falkland slept among the slain at night.

1831.

THE PATRIOT'S PASS-WORD.

On the achievement of Arnold de Winkelried, at the battle of Sempach, in which the Swiss insurgents secured the freedom of their country, against the power of Austria, in the fourteenth century.

"Make way for liberty!" he cried,
Made way for liberty, and died.

In arms the Austrian phalanx stood,
A living wall, a human wood;
A wall, — where every conscious stone
Seem'd to its kindred thousands grown,
A rampart all assaults to bear,
Till time to dust their frames should wear:
A wood, — like that enchanted grove *
In which with fiends Rinaldo strove,
Where every silent tree possess'd
A spirit imprison'd in its breast,
Which the first stroke of coming strife
Might startle into hideous life:
So still, so dense the Austrians stood,
A living wall, a human wood.
Impregnable their front appears,
All-horrent with projected spears,

* *Gerusalemme Liberata*, canto xviii.

Whose polish'd points before them shine,
From flank to flank, one brilliant line,
Bright as the breakers' splendors run
Along the billows to the sun.

Opposed to these, a hovering band
Contended for their father-land;
Peasants, whose new-found strength had broke
From manly necks the' ignoble yoke,
And beat their fetters into swords,
On equal terms to fight their lords,
And what insurgent rage had gain'd,
In many a mortal fray maintain'd.
Marshall'd once more, at freedom's call
They came to conquer or to fall,
Where he who conquer'd, he who fell,
Was deem'd a dead or living Tell;
Such virtue had that patriot breathed,
So to the soil his soul bequeathed,
That wheresoe'er his arrows flew,
Heroes in his own likeness grew,
And warriors sprang from every sod,
Which his awakening footstep trod.

And now the work of life and death
Hung on the passing of a breath;
The fire of conflict burn'd within,
The battle trembled to begin;
Yet while the Austrians held their ground,
Point for assault was nowhere found;

Where'er the' impatient Switzers gazed,
The' unbroken line of lances blazed;
That line 't were suicide to meet,
And perish at their tyrants' feet:
How could they rest within their graves,
To leave their homes the haunts of slaves?
Would they not feel their children tread,
With clanking chains, above their head?

It must not be; this day, this hour
Annihilates the' invader's power;
All Switzerland is in the field,
She will not fly, she cannot yield,
She must not fall; her better fate
Here gives her an immortal date.
Few were the numbers she could boast,
Yet every freeman was a host,
And felt as 't were a secret known,
That one should turn the scale alone,
While each unto himself was he,
On whose sole arm hung victory.

It did depend on one indeed;
Behold him, — Arnold Winkelried;
There sounds not to the trump of fame
The echo of a nobler name.
Unmark'd he stood amidst the throng,
In rumination deep and long,
Till you might see, with sudden grace,
The very thought come o'er his face,

And by the motion of his form
Anticipate the bursting storm,
And by the' uplifting of his brow
Tell where the bolt would strike, and how.

But 't was no sooner thought than done,
The field was in a moment won;
"Make way for liberty!" he cried,
Then ran, with arms extended wide,
As if his dearest friend to clasp;
Ten spears he swept within his grasp;
"Make way for liberty!" he cried,
Their keen points cross'd from side to side;
He bow'd amidst them, like a tree,
And thus made way for liberty.

Swift to the breach his comrades fly,
"Make way for liberty!" they cry,
And through the Austrian phalanx dart,
As rush'd the spears through Arnold's heart,
While, instantaneous as his fall,
Rout, ruin, panic seized them all;
An earthquake could not overthrow
A city with a surer blow.

Thus Switzerland again was free;
Thus death made way for liberty.

Redcar, 1827.

THE VOYAGE OF THE BLIND.

"It was that fatal and perfidious bark,
Built in the' eclipse, and rigg'd with curses dark."
MILTON'S *Lycidas.*

The subject of the following poem was suggested by certain well-authenticated facts, published at Paris, in a medical journal, some years ago; of which a few particulars may be given here.

"The ship *Le Rodeur*, Captain B., of two hundred tons' burden, left Havre on the 24th of January, 1819, for the coast of Africa, and reached her destination on the 14th of March following, anchoring at Bonny, on the river Calabar. The crew, consisting of twenty-two men, enjoyed good health during the outward voyage, and during their stay at Bonny, where they continued till the 6th of April. They had observed no trace of ophthalmia among the natives; and it was not until fifteen days after they had set sail on the return voyage, and the vessel was near the equator that they perceived the first symptoms of this frightful malady. It was then remarked, that the negroes, who, to the number of one hundred and sixty, were crowded together in the hold, and between the decks, had contracted a considerable redness of the eyes, which spread with singular rapidity. No great attention was at first paid to these symptoms, which were thought to be caused only by the want of air in the hold, and by the scarcity of water, which had already begun to be felt. At this time they were limited to eight ounces of water a day for each person, which quantity was afterwards reduced to the half of a wine-glass. By the advice of M. Maugnan, the surgeon of the ship, the negroes, who had hitherto remained shut up in the hold, were brought upon deck in succession, in order that they might breathe a purer air. But it became necessary to abandon this expedient, salutary as it was, because many of the negroes, affected with *nostalgia* (a passionate longing to return to their native land), threw themselves into the sea locked in each other's arms.

"The disease which had spread itself so rapidly and frightfully among the Africans, soon began to infect all on board. The danger also was greatly increased by a malignant dysentery which prevailed at the time. The first of the crew who caught it was a sailor who slept under the deck near the grated hatch which communicated with the hold. The next day a landsman was seized with ophthalmia; and in three days more the captain and the whole ship's company except one sailor, who remained at the helm, were blinded by the disorder.

"All means of cure which the surgeon employed, while he was able to act, proved ineffectual. The sufferings of the crew, which were otherwise intense, were aggravated by apprehension of revolt among the negroes, and the dread of not being able to reach the West Indies, if the only sailor who had hitherto escaped the contagion, and on whom their whole hope rested, should lose his sight like the rest. This calamity had actually befallen the *Leon*, a Spanish vessel which the Rodeur met on her passage, and the whole of whose crew, having become blind, were under the necessity of altogether abandoning the direction of their ship. These unhappy creatures, as they passed, earnestly entreated the charitable interference of the seamen of the Rodeur; but these, under their own affliction, could neither quit their vessel to go on board the Leon, nor receive the crew of the latter into the Rodeur, where, on account of the cargo of negroes, there was scarcely room for themselves. The vessels, therefore, soon parted company, and the Leon was never seen or heard of again, so far as could be traced at the publication of this narrative. In all probability, then, it was lost. On the fate of *this* vessel the poem is founded.

"The Rodeur reached Guadaloupe on the 21st of June, 1819; her crew being in a most deplorable condition. Of the negroes, thirty-seven had become perfectly blind, twelve had lost each an eye, and fourteen remained otherwise blemished by the disease. Of the crew, twelve, including the surgeon, had entirely lost their sight; five escaped with an eye each, and four were partially injured."

PART I.

O'er Africa the morning broke,
   And many a negro-land reveal'd,
From Europe's eye and Europe's yoke,
   In nature's inmost heart conceal'd:
Here roll'd the Nile his glittering train,
From Ethiopia to the main;
And Niger there uncoil'd his length,
That hides his fountain and his strength,
   Among the realms of noon;
Casting away their robes of night,

Forth stood in nakedness of light,
  The mountains of the moon.

Hush'd were the howlings of the wild,
  The leopard in his den lay prone;
Man, while creation round him smiled,
  Was sad or savage, man alone;
— Down in the dungeons of Algiers,
The Christian captive woke in tears;
— Caffraria's lean, marauding race
Prowl'd forth on pillage or the chase;
  — In Libyan solitude,
The' Arabian horseman scour'd along;
— The caravan's obstreperous throng,
  Their dusty march pursued.

But woe grew frantic in the west;
  A wily rover of the tide
Had mark'd the hour of Afric's rest,
  To snatch her children from her side:
At early dawn, to prospering gales,
The eager seamen stretch their sails;
The anchor rises from its sleep
Beneath the rocking of the deep;
  Impatient from the shore,
A vessel steals; — she steals away,
Mute as the lion with his prey,
  — A human prey *she* bore.

Curst was her trade and contraband,
  Therefore that keel, by guilty stealth,

Fled with the darkness from the strand,
  Laden with living bales of wealth:
Fair to the eye her streamers play'd
With undulating light and shade;
White from her prow the gurgling foam
Flew backward tow'rds the negro's home,
  Like his unheeded sighs;
Sooner that melting foam shall reach
His inland home, than yonder beach
  Again salute his eyes.

Tongue hath not language to unfold
  The secrets of the space between
That vessel's flanks, — whose dungeon-hold
  Hides what the sun hath never seen;
Three hundred writhing prisoners there
Breathe one mephitic blast of air
From lip to lip; — like flame suprest,
It bursts from every tortured breast,
  With dreary groans and strong;
Lock'd side to side, they feel by starts,
The beating of each other's hearts,
  — Their breaking too, ere long.

Light o'er the blue untroubled sea,
  Fancy might deem that vessel held
Her voyage to eternity,
  By one unchanging breeze impell'd;
— Eternity is in the sky,
Whose span of distance mocks the eye;

Eternity upon the main,
The horizon there is sought in vain;
  Eternity below
Appears in heaven's inverted face;
And on, through everlasting space,
  The' unbounded billows flow.

Yet, while his wandering bark career'd,
  The master knew, with stern delight,
That full for port her helm was steer'd,
  With aim unerring, day and night.
— Pirate! that port thou ne'er shalt hail;
Thine eye in search of it shall fail:
But, lo! thy slaves expire beneath;
Haste, bring the wretches forth to breathe:
  Brought forth, — away they spring,
And headlong in the whelming tide,
Rescued from thee, their sorrows hide
  Beneath the halcyon's wing.

PART II.

There came an angel of eclipse,
  Who haunts at times the' Atlantic flood,
And smites with blindness, on their ships,
  The captives and the men of blood.
— *Here*, in the hold the blight began,
From eye to eye contagion ran;

Sight, as with burning brands, was quench'd;
None from the fiery trial blench'd,
But, panting for release,
They call'd on death, who, close behind,
Brought pestilence to lead the blind,
From agony to peace.

The twofold plague no power could check;
Unseen its withering arrows flew;
It walk'd in silence on the deck,
And smote from stem to stern the crew:
— As glow-worms dwindle in the shade,
As lamps in charnel-houses fade,
From every orb, with vision fired,
In flitting sparks the light retired;
The sufferers saw it go,
And o'er the ship, the sea, the skies,
Pursued it with their failing eyes,
Till all was black below.

A murmur swell'd along the gale,
All rose, and held their breath to hear;
All look'd, but none could spy a sail,
Although a sail was near;
— "Help! help!" our beckoning sailors cried;
"'Help! help!'" a hundred tongues replied:
Then hideous clamor rent the air,
Questions and answers of despair:
Few words the mystery clear'd
The pest had found that second bark,

Where every eye but his was dark,
  Whose hand the vessel steer'd.

He, wild with panic, turn'd away,
  And thence his shrieking comrades bore;
From either ship the winds convey
  Farewells, that soon are heard no more:
— A calm of horror hush'd the waves;
Behold them! — merchant, seamen, slaves,
The blind, the dying, and the dead;
All help, all hope, for ever fled;
  Unseen, yet face to face!
Woe past, woe present, woe to come,
Held for a while each victim dumb,
  — Impaled upon his place.

It is not in the blood of man
  To crouch ingloriously to fate;
Nature will struggle while she can;
  Misfortune makes her children great;
The head which lightning hath laid low,
Is hallow'd by the noble blow:
The wretch who yields a felon's breath,
Emerges from the cloud of death,
  A spirit on the storm:
But virtue perishing unknown,
Watch'd by the eye of heaven alone,
  Is earth's least earthly form.

What were the scenes on board that bark?
  The tragedy which none beheld,

When (as the deluge bore the ark),
By power invisible impell'd,
The keel went blindfold through the surge,
Where stream might drift, or tempest urge;
— Plague, famine, thirst, their numbers slew,
And frenzy seized the hardier few
Who yet were spared to try
How everlasting are the pangs,
When life upon a moment hangs,
And death stands mocking by.

Imagination's daring glance
May pierce that vale of mystery,
As in the rapture of a trance,
Things which no eye hath seen to see;
And hear by fits along the gales,
Screams, maniac-laughter, hollow wails:
— They stand, they lie, above, beneath,
Groans of unpitied anguish breathe,
Tears unavailing shed;
Each, in abstraction of despair,
Seems to himself a hermit there,
Alive among the dead.

Yet respite, — respite from his woes,
Even here, the conscious sufferer feels;
Worn down by torture to repose,
Slumber the vanish'd world reveals:
— Ah! then the eyes, extinct in night,
Again behold the blessed light;

Ah! then the frame of rack'd disease
Lays its delighted limbs at ease;
  Swift to his own dear land,
The unfetter'd slave with shouts returns,
Hard by his dreaming tyrant burns
  At sight of Cuba's strand.

To blank reality they wake,
  In darkness opens every eye:
Peace comes;—the negro's heart-strings break,
  To him 't is more than life to die:
— How feels, how fares the man of blood?
In endless exile on the flood,
Rapt, as though fiends his vessel steer'd,
Things which he once believed and fear'd,
  — Then scorn'd as idle names, —
Death, judgment, conscience, hell conspire,
With thronging images of fire,
  To light up guilt in flames.

Who cried for mercy in that hour,
  And found it on the desert sea?
Who to the utmost grasp of power
  Wrestled with life's last enemy?
Who, Marius-like, defying fate,
(Marius on fallen Carthage) sate?
Who, through a hurricane of fears,
Clung to the hopes of future years?
  And who, with heart unquail'd,
Look'd from time's trembling precipice

Down on eternity's abyss,
  Till breath and footing fail'd?

Is there among this crew not one,
  — One whom a widow'd mother bare, —
Who mourns far off her only son,
  And pours for him her soul in prayer?
Even *now*, when o'er his soften'd thought,
Remembrance of her love is brought,
To soothe death's agony, and dart
A throb of comfort through his heart, —
  Even *now* a mystic knell
Sounds through *her* pulse; — she lifts her eye,
Sees a pale spirit passing by,
  And hears *his* voice, "farewell!"

Mother and son shall meet no more:
  — The floating tomb of its own dead,
That ship shall never reach a shore;
  But, far from track of seamen led,
The sun shall watch it, day by day,
Careering on its lonely way;
Month after month, the moon shine pale
On falling mast and riven sail;
  The stars, from year to year,
Mark the bulged flanks, and sunken deck,
Till not a ruin of the wreck
  On ocean's face appear.

1820.

AN EVERY-DAY TALE.

Written for a benevolent Society in the metropolis, the object of which is to relieve poor women during *the first month of their widowhood*, to preserve what little property they may have from wreck and ruin, in a season of embarrassment, when kindness and good counsel are especially needed; and, so far as may be practicable, to assist the destitute with future means of maintaining themselves and their fatherless children.

"The short and simple annals of the poor." GRAY.

MINE is a tale of every day,
Yet turn not thou thine ear away;
For 't is the bitterest thought of all,
The wormwood *added* to the gall,
That such a wreck of mortal bliss,
That such a weight of woe as this,
Is no strange thing, — but, strange to say!
The tale, the truth of every day.

At Mary's birth, her mother smiled
Upon her first, last, only child,
And, at the sight of that young flower,
Forgot the anguish of her hour;
Her pains return'd; — she soon forgot
Love, joy, hope, sorrow, — she was not.

Her partner stood, like one bereft
Of all; — not all, their babe was left:

By the dead mother's side it slept,
Slept sweetly; — when it woke, it wept.
" Live, Mary, live, and I will be
Father and mother both to thee!"
The mourner cried, and while he spake,
His breaking heart forebore to break;
Faith, courage, patience, from above,
Flew to the help of fainting love.
While o'er his charge that parent yearn'd,
All woman's tenderness he learn'd,
All woman's waking, sleeping care,
— That sleeps not to her babe, — her prayer,
Of power to bring upon its head,
The richest blessings heaven can shed;
All these he learn'd, and lived to say,
" My strength was given me as my day."

So the Red Indian of those woods,
That echo to lake Erie's floods,
Reft of his consort in the wild,
Became the mother of his child!
Nature (herself a mother) saw
His grief, and loosed her kindliest law:
Warm from its fount life's stream, propell'd,
His breasts with sweet nutrition swell'd,
At whose strange springs, his infant drew
Milk, as the rose-bud drinks the dew.

Mary from childhood rose to youth,
In paths of innocence and truth;

—Train'd by her parent, from her birth,
To go to heaven by way of earth,
She was to him, in after-life,
Both as a daughter and a wife.

Meekness, simplicity, and grace,
Adorn'd her speech, her air, her face;
The spirit, through its earthly mould,
Broke, as the lily's leaves unfold;
Her beauty open'd on the sight,
As a star trembles into light.

Love found that maiden; love will find
Way to the coyest maiden's mind;
Love found and tried her many a year,
With hope deferr'd, and boding fear;
To the world's end her hero stray'd;
Tempests and calms his bark delay'd;
What then could her heart-sickness soothe?
"The course of true love ne'er ran smooth!"
Her bosom ached with drear suspense,
Till sharper trouble drove it thence:
Affliction smote her father's brain,
And he became a child again.
Ah! then, the prayers, the pangs, the tears,
He breathed, felt, shed on her young years,
That duteous daughter well repaid,
Till in the grave she saw him laid,
Beneath her mother's church-yard stone:
—*There* first she felt herself alone;

But while she gazed on that cold heap,
Her parents' bed, and could not weep,
A still small whisper seem'd to say,
"Strength shall be given thee as thy day:"
Then rush'd the tears to her relief;
A bow was in the cloud of grief.

Her wanderer now, from clime to clime,
Return'd, unchanged by tide or time,
True as the morning to the sun;
— Mary and William soon were one;
And never rang the village bells
With sweeter falls or merrier swells,
Than while the neighbors, young and old,
Stood at their thresholds, to behold,
And bless them, till they reach'd the spot,
Where woodbines girdled Mary's cot,
Where throstles, perch'd on orchard trees,
Sang to the hum of garden bees:
And there — no longer forced to roam —
William found all the world at home;
Yea more than all the world beside,
— A warm, kind heart to his allied.

Twelve years of humble life they spent,
With food and raiment well content;
In flower of youth and flush of health,
They envied not voluptuous wealth;
The wealth of poverty was theirs,
— Those riches without wings or snares,

Which honest hands, by daily toil,
May dig from every generous soil.
A little farm, while William till'd,
Mary her household cares fulfill'd;
And love, joy, peace, with guileless mirth,
Sate round their table, warm'd their hearth:
Whence rose, like incense, to the skies,
Morning and evening sacrifice,
And contrite spirits found, in prayer,
That home was heaven, for God was there.

Meanwhile the May-flowers on their lands
Were yearly pluck'd by younger hands;
New comers watch'd the swallows float,
And mock'd the cuckoo's double note;
Till, head o'er head, in slanting line,
They stood, — a progeny of nine,
That *might* be ten; — but ere that day,
The father's life was snatch'd away:
Faint from the field one night he came;
Fever had seized his sinewy frame,
And left the strong man, when it pass'd,
Frail as the sere leaf in the blast;
A long, long winter's illness, bow'd
His head; — spring-daisies deck'd his shroud.
Oh! 't was a bitter day for all,
The husband's, father's funeral;
The dead, the living, and the unborn
Met there, — were there asunder torn.

Scarce was he buried out of sight,
Ere his tenth infant sprang to light,
And Mary, from her child-bed throes,
To instant, utter ruin rose;
Harvests had fail'd, and sickness drain'd
Her frugal stock-purse, long retain'd;
Rents, debts, and taxes all fell due,
Claimants were loud, resources few,
Small, and remote; — yet time and care
Her shatter'd fortunes might repair,
If but a friend, — a friend in need, –
Such friend would be a friend indeed, —
Would, by a mite of succor lent,
Wrongs irretrievable prevent!
She look'd around for such an one,
And sigh'd but spake not, —"*Is there none?*"
— Oh! if he come not ere an hour,
All will elapse beyond her power,
And homeless, helpless, hopeless, lost,
Mary on this cold world be tost
With all her babes! * * * * *

Came such a friend? — I must not say;
Mine is a tale of every day:
But wouldst thou know the worst of all,
The wormwood mingled with the gall,
Go visit thou, in their distress,
The widow and the fatherless,
And thou shalt find such woe as this,
Such breaking up of earthly bliss,

Is no strange thing, — but, strange to say!
The tale — the truth — of every day.

Go, visit *thou*, in their distress,
The Widow and the Fatherless.

1830.

A TALE WITHOUT A NAME.

"O woman! in our hours of ease,
Uncertain, coy, and hard to please;
— When pain and anguish wring the brow,
A ministering angel thou!"
SCOTT'S *Marmion*, canto vi.

PART I.

HE had no friend on earth but thee;
No hope in heaven above;
By day and night, o'er land and sea,
No solace but thy love;
He wander'd here, he wander'd there,
A fugitive like Cain;
And mourn'd like him, in dark despair,
A brother rashly slain.

Rashly, yet not in sudden wrath,
They quarrell'd in their pride,
He sprang upon his brother's path,
And smote him that he died.
A nightmare sat upon his brain,
All stone within he felt;
A death-watch tick'd through every vein,
Till the dire blow was dealt.

As from a dream, in pale surprise,
  Waking, the murderer stood;
He met the victim's closing eyes,
  He saw his brother's blood:
That blood pursued him on his way,
  A living, murmuring stream;
Those eyes before him flash'd dismay,
  With ever-dying gleam.

In vain he strove to fly the scene,
  And breathe beyond that time;
Tormented memory glared between;
  Immortal seem'd his crime:
His thoughts, his words, his actions all
  Turn'd on his fallen brother;
That hour he never could recall,
  Nor ever live another.

To him the very clouds stood still,
  The ground appear'd unchanged;
One light was ever on the hill,
  — That hill where'er he ranged:
He heard the brook, the birds, the wind,
  Sound in the glen below;
The self-same tree he cower'd behind,
  He struck the self-same blow.

Yet was not reason quite o'erthrown,
  Nor so benign his lot,
To dwell in frenzied grief alone,
  All other woe forgot:

The world within and world around,
  Clash'd in perpetual strife;
Present and past close interwound
  Through his whole thread of life.

That thread, inextricably spun,
  Might reach eternity;
For ever doing, never done,
  That moment's deed might be;
This was a worm that would not die,
  A fire unquenchable:
Ah! whither shall the sufferer fly?
  Fly from a bosom-hell?

He had no friend on earth but thee,
  No hope in heaven above;
By day and night, o'er land and sea,
  No refuge but thy love;
Not time nor place, nor crime nor shame,
  Could change thy spousal truth;
In desolate old age the same
  As in the joy of youth.

Not death, but infamy, to 'scape,
  He left his native coast;
To death in any other shape,
  He long'd to yield the ghost:
But infamy his steps pursued,
  And haunted every place,
While death, though like a lover wooed,
  Fled from his loathed embrace.

He wander'd here, he wander'd there,
   And she his angel-guide, —
The silent spectre of despair,
   With mercy at his side;
Whose love and loveliness alone
   Shed comfort round his gloom,
— Pale as the monumental stone
   That watches o'er a tomb.

PART II.

They cross'd the blue Atlantic flood;
   A storm their bark assail'd;
Stern through the hurricane he stood,
   All hearts, all efforts fail'd:
With horrid hope, he eyed the waves,
   That flash'd like wild-fires dim:
But ocean, 'midst a thousand graves,
   Denied a grave to him.

On shore he sought delirious rest,
   In crowds of busy men,
When suddenly the yellow pest
   Came reeking from its den:
The city vanish'd at its breath;
   He caught the taint, and lay
A suppliant at the gate of death,
   — Death spurn'd the wretch away.

In solitude of streams and rocks,
  Mountains and forests dread,
Where nature's free and fearless flocks
  At her own hand are fed,
They hid their pangs; — but oh! to live
  In peace, — in peace to die, —
Was more than solitude could give,
  Or earth's whole round supply.

The swampy wilderness their haunt,
  Where fiery panthers prowl,
Serpents their fatal splendors flaunt,
  And wolves and lynxes howl;
Where alligators throng the floods,
  And reptiles, venom-arm'd,
Infest the air, the fields, the woods,
  They slept, they waked unharm'd.

Where the Red Indians, in their ire,
  With havoc mark the way,
Skulk in dark ambush, waste with fire,
  Or gorge inhuman prey:
Their blood no wild marauder shed;
  Secure without defence,
Alike, were his devoted head,
  And her meek innocence.

Weary of loneliness, they turn'd
  To Europe's carnage-field;
At glory's Moloch-shrine, he burn'd
  His hated breath to yield:

He plunged into the hottest strife;
He dealt the deadliest blows;
To every foe exposed his life;
Powerless were all his foes.

The iron thunder-bolts, with wings
Of lightning, shunn'd his course;
Harmless the hail of battle rings,
The bayonet spends its force;
The sword to smite him flames aloof,
Descends,—but strikes in vain;
His branded front was weapon-proof,
He wore the mark of Cain.

"I cannot live,—I cannot die!"
He mutter'd in despair;
"This curse of immortality,
O, could I quit,—or bear!"
—Of every frantic hope bereft,
To meet a nobler doom,
One refuge,—only one, was left,—
To storm the' unyielding tomb.

Through his own breast the passage lay,
The steel was in his hand;
But fiends upstarting fenced the way,
And every nerve unmann'd:
The heart that ached its blood to spill,
With palsying horror died;
The arm, rebellious to his will,
Hung withering at his side.

O, woman! wonderful in love,
  Whose weakness is thy power,
How did thy spirit rise above
  The conflict of that hour!
— She found him prostrate; — not a sigh
  Escaped her tortured breast,
Nor fell one tear-drop from her eye,
  Where torrents were supprest.

Her faithful bosom stay'd his head,
  That throbb'd with fever heat;
Her eye serene compassion shed,
  Which his could never meet:
Her arms enclasp'd his shuddering frame,
  While at his side she kneel'd,
And utter'd nothing but his name,
  Yet all her soul reveal'd.

Touch'd to the quick, he gave no sign
  By gentle word or tone;
In him affection could not shine,
  'T was fire within a stone;
Which no collision by the way
  Could startle into light,
Though the poor heart that held it, lay
  Wrapt in Cimmerian night.

It was not always thus; — erewhile
  The kindness of his youth,
His brow of innocence, and smile
  Of unpretending truth, —

Had left such strong delight, — that she
  Would oft recall the time,
And live in golden memory,
  Unconscious of his crime.

Though self-abandon'd now to fate,
  The passive prey of grief,
Sullen, and cold, and desolate,
  He shunn'd, he spurn'd relief:
Still onward in its even course
  Her pure affection press'd,
And pour'd with soft and silent force
  Its sweetness through his breast.

Thus Sodom's melancholy lake
  No turn or current knows;
Nor breeze, nor billow sounding, break
  The horror of repose;
While Jordan, through the sulphurous brine,
  Rolls a translucent stream,
Whose waves with answering beauty shine
  To every changing beam.

PART III.

At length the hardest trial came,
  Again they cross the seas;
The waves their wilder fury tame,
  The storm becomes a breeze:

Homeward their easy course they hold,
  And now in radiant view,
The purple forelands, tinged with gold,
  Larger and lovelier grew.

The vessel on the tranquil tide
  Then seem'd to lie at rest,
While Albion, in maternal pride,
  Advanced with open breast
To bid them welcome on the main:
  — Both shrunk from her embrace;
Cold grew the pulse through every vein;
  He turn'd away his face.

Silent, apart, on deck he stands
  In ecstasy of woe;
A brother's blood is on his hands,
  He sees, he hears it flow:
Wilder than ocean tempest-wrought,
  Though deadly calm his look;
— His partner read his inmost thought,
  And strength her limbs forsook.

Then first, then last, a pang she proved
  Too exquisite to bear:
She fell, — he caught her, — strangely moved.
  Roused from intense despair;
Alive to feelings long unknown,
  He wept upon her cheek,
And call'd her in as kind a tone
  As love's own lips could speak.

Her spirit heard that voice, and felt
  Arrested on its flight;
Back to the mansion where it dwelt,
  Back from the gates of light,
That open'd paradise in trance,
  It hasten'd from afar,
Quick as the startled seaman's glance
  Turns from the polar star.

She breathed again, look'd up, and lo!
  Those eyes that knew not tears,
With streams of tenderness o'erflow;
  That heart, through hopeless years,
The den of fiends in darkness chain'd,
  That would not, dared not rest,
Affection fervent, pure, unfeign'd,
  In speechless sighs express'd.

Content to live, since now she knew
  What love believed before;
Content to live, since he was true,
  And love could ask no more,—
This vow to righteous heaven she made,
  —"Whatever ills befall,
Patient, unshrinking, undismay'd,
  I'll freely suffer all."

They land,—they take the wonted road,
  By twice ten years estranged;
The trees, the fields, their old abode,
  Objects and men had changed:

Familiar faces, forms endear'd,
  Each well-remember'd name,
From earth itself had disappear'd,
  Or seem'd no more the same.

The old were dead, the young were old;
  Children to men had sprung;
And every eye to them was cold,
  And silent every tongue;
Friendless, companionless, they roam
  Amidst their native scene;
In drearier banishment at home,
  Than savage climes had been.

PART IV.

Yet worse she fear'd; — nor long they lay
  In safety or suspense;
Unslumbering justice seized her prey,
  And dragg'd the culprit thence:
Amid the dungeons darken'd walls,
  Down on the cold damp floor,
A wreck of misery he falls,
  Close to the bolted door.

And she is gone, — while he remains,
  Bewilder'd in the gloom,
To brood in solitude and chains
  Upon a felon's doom:

Yes she is gone, — and he forlorn
  Must groan the night away,
And long to see her face at morn,
  More welcome than the day.

The morning comes, — she reappears
  With grief-dissembling wiles;
A sad serenity of tears,
  An agony of smiles,
Her looks assume; his spectral woes
  Are vanish'd at the sight;
And all within him seem'd repose,
  And all around him light.

Never since that mysterious hour,
  When kindred blood was spilt, —
Never had aught in nature power
  To soothe corroding guilt,
Till the glad moment when she cross'd
  The threshold of that place,
And the wild rapture, when he lost
  Himself in her embrace.

Even then, while on her neck he hung,
  Ere yet a word they spoke,
As by a fiery serpent stung,
  Away at once he broke:
Frenzy, remorse, confusion, burst
  In tempest o'er his brain;
He felt accused, condemn'd, accurst,
  He was himself again.

Days, weeks, and months, had mark'd the flight
  Of time's unwearied wing,
Ere winter's long, lugubrious night
  Relented into spring:
To him who pined for death's release,
  An age the space between!
To her who could not hope for peace,
  How fugitive the scene!

In vain she chid forewarning fears,
  In vain repress'd her woe,
Alone, unseen, her sighs and tears
  Would freely heave and flow:
Yet ever in his sight, by day,
  Her looks were calm and kind,
And when at evening torn away,
  She left her soul behind.

Hark! — hark! — the Judge is at the gate,
  The trumpets' thrilling tones
Ring through the cells, the voice of fate!
  Reëchoed thence in groans:
The sound hath reach'd her ear, — she stands,
  In marble chillness dumb;
He too hath heard, and smites his hands:
  "I come," he cried, "I come."

Before the dread tribunal now,
  Firm in collected pride,
Without a scowl upon his brow,
  Without a pang to hide,

He stood; — superior in that hour
  To recreant fear and shame;
Peril itself inspired the power
  To meet the worst that came.

'T was like the tempest when he sought
  Fate in the swallowing flood;
'T was like the battle, when he fought
  For death through seas of blood:
— A violence which soon must break
  The heart that would not bend,
— A heart that almost ceased to ache
  In hope of such an end.

On him, while every eye was fix'd,
  And every lip express'd,
Without a voice, the rage unmix'd,
  That boil'd in every breast;
It seem'd, as though that deed abhorr'd,
  In years far distant done,
Had cut asunder every cord
  Of fellowship but one, —

That *one* indissolubly bound
  A feeble woman's heart:
— Faithful in every trial found,
  Long had she borne her part;
Now at his helpless side alone,
  Girt with infuriate crowds,
Like the new moon her meekness shone,
  Pale through a gulf of clouds.

Ah! well might every bosom yearn,
  Responsive to her sigh;
And every visage, dark and stern,
  Soften beneath that eye:
Ah! well might every lip of gall,
  The unutter'd curse suspend;
Its tones for her in blessings fall,
  Its breath in prayer ascend.

"Guilty!" — that thunder-striking sound,
  All shudder'd when they heard;
A burst of horrid joy around
  Hail'd the tremendous word;
Check'd in a moment, — *she* was there!
  The instinctive groan was hush'd;
Nature, that forced it, cried, — "Forbear;"
  Indignant justice blush'd.

PART V.

One woe is past, another speeds
  To brand and seal his doom;
The third day's failing beam recedes,
  She watch'd it into gloom:
That night, how swift in its career,
  It flew from sun to sun!
That night, the last of many a dear,
  And many a dolorous one! —

That night, by special grace she wakes
   In the lone convict's cell,
With him for whom the morrow breaks,
   To light to heaven or hell:
Dread sounds of preparation rend
   The dungeon's ponderous roof;
The hammer's doubling strokes descend,
   The scaffold creaks aloof.

She watch'd his features through the shade,
   Which glimmering embers broke;
Both from their inmost spirit pray'd;
   They pray'd, but seldom spoke:
Moments meanwhile were years to him;
   Her grief forgot their flight,
Till on the hearth the fire grew dim;
   She turn'd, and lo! the light;—

The light less welcome to her eyes,
   The loveliest light of morn,
Than the dark glare of felons' eyes
   Through grated cells forlorn:
The cool fresh breeze from heaven that blew,
   The free lark's mounting strains,
She felt in drops of icy dew,
   She heard, like groans and chains.

"Farewell!"—'t was but a word, yet more
   Was utter'd in that sound,
Than love had ever told before,
   Or sorrow yet had found:

They kiss like meeting flames, — they part,
Like flames asunder driven;
Lip cleaves to lip, heart beats on heart
Till soul from soul is riven.

Quick hurried thence, — the sullen bell
Its pausing peal began;
She hearkens, — 'tis the dying knell,
Rung for the living man:
The mourner reach'd her lonely bower,
Fell on her widow'd bed,
And found, through one entrancing hour,
The quiet of the dead.

She woke, — and knew he was no more:
"Thy dream of life is past;
That pang with thee, that pang is o'er,
The bitterest and the last!"
She cried: — then scenes of sad amaze
Flash'd on her inward eye;
A field, a troop, a crowd to gaze,
A murderer led to die!

He eyed the ignominious tree,
Look'd round, but saw no friend;
Was plunged into eternity;
— Is this — is this the end?
Her spirit follow'd him afar
Into the world unknown,
And saw him standing at that bar,
Where each must stand alone.

Silence and darkness hide the rest
— Long she survived to mourn;
But peace sprang up within her breast,
From trouble meekly borne:
And higher, holier joys had she,
A Christian's hopes above,
The prize of suffering constancy,
The crown of faithful love.

1821.

A SNAKE IN THE GRASS.

A TALE FOR CHILDREN: FOUNDED ON FACTS.

SHE had a secret of her own,
  That little girl of whom we speak,
O'er which she oft would muse alone,
  Till the blush came across her cheek,
A rosy cloud, that glow'd awhile,
Then melted in a sunny smile.

There was so much to charm the eye,
  So much to move delightful thought,
Awake at night she loved to lie,
  Darkness to her that image brought;
She murmur'd of it in her dreams,
Like the low sounds of gurgling streams.

What secret thus the soul possess'd
  Of one so young and innocent?
Oh! nothing but a robin's nest,
  O'er which in ecstasy she bent;
That treasure she herself had found,
With five brown eggs, upon the ground.

When first it flash'd upon her sight,
  Bolt flew the dam above her head;

She stoop'd, and almost shriek'd with fright;
But spying soon that little bed
With feathers, moss, and horse-hairs twined,
Rapture and wonder fill'd her mind.

Breathless and beautiful she stood,
Her ringlets o'er her bosom fell;
With hands uplift, in attitude,
As though a pulse might break the spell,
While through the shade her pale, fine face
Shone like a star amidst the place.

She stood so silent, stay'd so long,
The parent-birds forgot their fear;
Cock-robin trill'd his small, sweet song,
In notes like dew-drops trembling, clear;
From spray to spray the shyer hen
Dropt softly on her nest again.

There Lucy mark'd her slender bill
On this side, and on that her tail,
Peer'd o'er the edge, — while, fix'd and still,
Two bright black eyes her own assail,
Which, in eye language, seem'd to say,
"Peep, pretty maiden! then, away!"

Away, away at length she crept,
So pleased, she knew not how she trode,
Yet light on tottering tiptoe stept,
As if birds' eggs strew'd all the road;

With folded arms, and lips compress'd,
To keep her joy within her breast.

Morn, noon, and eve, from day to day,
By stealth she visited that spot:
Alike her lessons and her play
Were slightly conn'd, or half forgot;
And when the callow young were hatch'd,
With infant fondness Lucy watch'd:—

Watch'd the kind parents dealing food
To clamorous suppliants all agape;
Watch'd the small, naked, unform'd brood
Improve in size, and plume, and shape,
Till feathers clad the fluttering things,
And the whole group seem'd bills and wings.

Unconsciously within her breast,
Where many a brooding fancy lay,
She plann'd to bear the tiny nest,
And chirping choristers away,
In stately cage to tune their throats,
And learn untaught their mother-notes.

One morn, when fairly fledged for flight,
Blithe Lucy, on her visit, found
What seem'd a necklace, glittering bright,
Twined round the nest, twined round and round,
With emeralds, pearls, and sapphires set,
Rich as my lady's coronet.

She stretch'd her hand to seize the prize,
  When up a serpent popt its head,
But glid like wild-fire from her eyes,
  Hissing and rustling as it fled;
She utter'd one short shrilling scream,
Then stood, as startled from a dream.

Her brother Tom, who long had known
  That something drew her feet that way,
Curious to catch her there alone,
  Had follow'd her that fine May-day;
— Lucy, bewilder'd by her trance,
Came to herself at his first glance.

Then in her eyes sprang welcome tears;
  They fell as showers in April fall;
He kiss'd her, coax'd her, soothed her fears,
  Till she in frankness told him all:
— Tom was a bold, adventurous boy,
And heard the dreadful tale with joy.

For he had learnt, — in some far land, —
  How children catch the sleeping snake;
Eager himself to try his hand,
  He cut a hazel from the brake,
And like a hero set to work,
To make a lithe, long-handled fork.

Brother and sister then withdrew,
  Leaving the nestlings safely there;

Between their heads the mother flew,
  Prompt to resume her nursery care:
But Tom, whose breast for glory burn'd,
In less than half an hour return'd.

With him came Ned, as cool and sly
  As Tom was resolute and stout;
So fair and softly, they drew nigh,
  Cowering and keeping sharp look-out,
Till they had reach'd the copse, — to see,
But not alarm the enemy.

Guess, with what transport they descried,
  How, as before, the serpent lay
Coil'd round the nest, in slumbering pride; —
  The urchins chuckled o'er their prey,
And Tom's right hand was lifted soon,
Like Greenland whaler's with harpoon.

Across its neck the fork he brought,
  And pinn'd it fast upon the ground;
The reptile woke, and quick as thought
  Curl'd round the stick, curl'd round and round:
While, head and tail, Ned's nimble hands
Tied at each end, with pack-thread bands.

Scarce was the enemy secured,
  When Lucy timidly drew near,
But by their shouting well assured,
  Eyed the green captive void of fear;

The lads, stark wild with victory, flung
Their caps aloft, — they danced, they sung.

But Lucy, with an anxious look,
  Turn'd to her own dear nest, when lo!
To legs and wings the young ones took,
  Hopping and tumbling to and fro;
The parents chattering from above
With all the earnestness of love.

Alighting now among their train,
  They peck'd them on new feats to try;
But many a lesson seem'd in vain,
  Before the giddy things would fly:
Lucy both laugh'd and cried, to see
How ill they play'd at liberty.

I need not tell the snake's sad doom,
  You may be sure he lived not long;
Cork'd in a bottle for a tomb,
  Preserved in spirits and in song,
His skin in Tom's museum shines,
You read his story in these lines.

1831.

TRANSLATIONS FROM DANTE.

TRANSLATIONS FROM DANTE.

UGOLINO AND RUGGIERI.

The sufferings of Ugolino on earth, and his cannibal revenge in hell, on his betrayer and murderer, Ruggieri, are better known in this country than any other part of the Divina Commedia, having been often translated, and several times made the subject of painting, especially in the rival pictures of Reynolds and Fuseli. One version more may be tolerated, and it will probably be long before it can be said that yet another is not wanted, to give the English reader an adequate idea of the poet's power in the delineation, — not so much of the supernatural horrors of his infernal caverns, as of a real earthly scene (like the death by starvation in the dungeon of a father and his four innocent children), "so simply, so severely great," that of the narrative, in his own Italian, it may be said,

"The force of nature could no further go."

Ugolino, Count of Gherardesca, having united with the Archbishop Ruggieri degli Ubaldini to expel his own nephew, Nino Giudice di Gallura from the sovereignty of Pisa, seized it for himself. But the archbishop soon turned against him, and being supported by Laufranchi, Sismondi, and Gualandi, three of the principal inhabitants, they raised a tumult in the city, during which Ugolino was dragged from his palace, and with his two sons, and their two sons (he calls all four his children in the story), imprisoned in a tower on the Piazza degli Anziani, for several months, at the expiration of which the portals were all locked, and the keys thrown into the river Arno: the miserable captives being thus left to perish with hunger, whence the hold itself obtained the name of "*Famine*." With great skill, to produce the most pathetic impression, as well as with consummate knowledge of human nature, Dante makes Ugolino dwell wholly on the treachery and cruelty exercised towards himself, without any allusion to his own atrocious injustice towards his nephew, for which he is doomed to the second round of the ninth or lowest gulf of Hell, with no mitigation of the pains of eternal hunger, except the ravenous feast, like that of the eagle on the liver of Prometheus, upon the never-satisfying and never-wasting brain of the traitor Ruggieri

Dante (accompanied by Virgil, his conductor,) finds in this department of "the doleful city" the victims tormented variously, according to their crimes,

"In thrilling regions of thick-ribbed ice;"

and, among others, the two personages aforenamed.

SCARCE had we parted thence, when I beheld
Two in one well of ice, so grouped together
The head of one to the other seem'd the cowl,
While, like a hungry man devouring bread,
The uppermost had fasten'd with his teeth
Upon the lower, where skull and neck are join'd;
Nor more voraciously did Tydeus tear
The front of Menalippus, in his rage,*
Than on that head and brain the' assailant prey'd.

"O thou!" I cried, "who show'st by such brute token
Hatred to him whom thou devourest, say,
Why dost thou so? — I ask on this condition,
That knowing who thou art, and what his crime,
If thou have cause of wrong against thy victim,
I yet may right thee in the upper world,
Should *that* with which I speak be not dried up."
Dell' Inferno, canto xxxii.

The sinner paused amidst his dire repast,
And wiped his mouth upon the hairy scalp

* STATIUS, *Theb.* l. vii.

Of him whose head he raven'd on behind,
Then answer'd: —
"Thou wouldst have me to renew
Horrible pangs, of which the very thought
So wrings my heart, I scarce find power for utterance:
Yet if my words prove seed, of which the traitor,
Whom thus I gnaw, may reap the' accursed fruit,
Thou shalt behold me weep and speak at once.

"I know not who thou art, nor by what means
Thou hast come hither, but a Florentine,
By speech, I deem thee. — Know me, then, [thee,
Count Ugolino, — this, the' Archbishop Ruggier,
And why I'm such a neighbor thou shalt hear.
— I need not say how, by his foul devices,
Reposing on his faith, I was ensnared,
And murder'd: — but, what cannot have been told
How cruel was that murder, thou shalt know;
Then judge if he have injured me or not.

"When the small casement of that dungeon cage,
Which hath from me the name of 'Famine,' — where
Others may yet be left like me to perish, —
Through its dim aperture, had more than once
Shown the new moon, an evil sleep fell on me,
Which from the future rent the veil.
— Methought
This wretch, as lord and master of the field,
Hunted a he-wolf and his whelps along
The mountain which from Pisa shadows Lucca.

With meagre, staunch, and noble-blooded hounds,
Gualandi, and Sismondi, and Lanfranchi
Swept on before him. — After a short chase,
Parent and young fell, fainting from fatigue,
And with keen fangs I saw them torn to pieces.

"When I awoke at daybreak, — in their sleep,
I heard my children moan, and ask for bread
(For they were with me); — cruel is thine heart
If it grieves not for what mine then foreboded,
And if thou weep'st not now, what wilt thou weep for?
— Ere long they woke; the hour drew nigh when food
Was wont to be brought to us; but in each
Secret misgivings from his dream arose;
And of the horrible tower, I heard the portal
Lock'd underneath our cell. Thereat I look'd
Full on my children, but spake not a word,
Nor wept, so petrified I felt within.
They wept, and little Anselm said to me,
'You look so, father! Ah! what mean those looks?'
Still I wept not, nor answer'd all that day,
Nor the next night.
At sunrise on the morrow,
When a faint ray gleam'd through our doleful prison,
And in four haggard faces show'd me mine,
I worried both my hands with agony:
They, thinking that I did so in the rage
Of hunger, all together rose and cried,
'Father! 't will hurt us less if you will feed

On us; you clothed these limbs with suffering flesh,
Now strip them!'
Then I quieted myself,
Not to make them more wretched. — All that day,
And all the next, we sat, and held our peace;
Ah! earth, hard earth! why didst thou not then open?

"When we had linger'd on till the fourth day,
My Gaddo threw himself down at my feet,
Crying, 'My father! why do you not help me?'
Then died. — As plainly as thou seest me now,
I saw the other three fall, one by one,
Between the fifth day and the sixth. Then blind
I groped about to feel and clasp their bodies;
Three days I call'd them by their names, though dead,
Then famine did for me what grief could not."

Dell' Inferno, canto xxxiii.

MAESTRO ADAMO.

The hideously comic interview and adventure with Maestro Adamo (Master Adam), the coiner, — in another of the lower rounds of the infernal gulf, where traitors of the baser sort are tormented with unappeasable thirst, in various diseases that excite it, – is thoroughly *Dantesque*, but in the poet's coarser vein. It may form a singular companion-piece to the fearfully sublime, but simply told and tenderly affecting, narrative of Count Ugolino.

I SAW one shapen like a lute, had he
Been shorten'd where the man becomes a fork; *
Enormous dropsy (which had swoln his limbs
With stagnant humors, till his ghastly cheek
But ill agreed with his unwieldy paunch,)
Made him, for thirst, gasp like a hectic, — one
Lip lolling on his chin, upcurl'd the other.

"Oh! you," he cried, "that without pain (though why
I know not) pass through this unhappy world,
Hear, and mark well the sorrows of Adāmo;
Living, I had whatever heart could wish,
And now, alas! I lack a drop of water.
The murmuring rivulets down the verdant hill

* The strange phrase employed in the original quaintly signifies,
— "if he had been shortened from the waist."

Of Cassentino, flowing into Arno,
Which keep their little channels moist and cool,
Are ever in mine eye ; — and not in vain,
For their sweet images inflame my thirst
More than the malady that shrinks my visage.
The rigid justice, which torments me here,
Even from the place where I committed sin,
Draws means to mock and multiply my groans ;
Romena stands before me, where I forged
The lawful coin and Baptist's seal, for which
I left my wretched body in the flames.*
— Yet could I spy the woeful ghost of Guido,
Of Alessandro, or their brother, here,
I would not quit the sight for Brandra's fountain !
Somewhere among these pits dwells one, — if truth
Be told by those mad souls that roam at large, —
But what is that to me whose limbs are bound ?
Oh ! were I light enough to move an inch
A century, I had set out ere now
In search of him among the hideous throng,
Through all the eleven long miles of this sad circle,
Which hath not less than half a mile in breadth !
They brought me to this family of fiends,
They tempted me to falsify the florin,
And mix it with three carats of alloy."

* This miserable culprit had been a metallurgist of Brescia, who, at the instance of Guido, Alessandro, and Aginulpho, three nobles of Romena, counterfeited the gold florin of Tuscany, which bore the impress of the Baptist's head. — Branda is a beautiful fountain at Siena.

Then I to him: — "And who are these two wretches, [snow,
That smoke like hands in winter plunged through
Lying close fetter'd on the right of thee?"

"I found them here, and they have never stirr'd
Since I was dropt into this ditch," he answer'd;
"One's the false woman who accused young Joseph,
And t'other Sinon, the false Greek at Troy,
Who, in the excruciate pangs of putrid fever,
Send up such steam."

That moment one of them,
Wroth to be named so ignominiously,
Struck with the fist on his distended hide,
That thunder'd like a drum; — but Master Adam
Repaid the blow upon the assailant's face,
Not less afflictive, with his arm; exclaiming,
"Though reft of locomotion, being so large,
I have a hand at liberty for *that*."

To whom the other: — "Thou wert not so prompt,
When thou wast going to the stake; and yet
More prompt than now when thou didst stamp the coin."

"Thou speak'st the truth," the dropsical replied,
"But not so at Troy, when truth was ask'd thee."

"False words I utter'd then, as thou false money;

If for one crime I suffer, thou art damn'd
For more than any demon here," quoth Sinon.

"Remember! perjured one, the hollow horse,
With its full belly," Adam cried, "and stand
Guilty through all the world."

"Stand guilty thou!"
The Greek retorted; "witness that huge round,
That quagmire, which ingulfs thee in thyself."

The coiner then:—"Thy mouth for evilspeaking
Is quite as open as it wont to be;
If I have drought while humors swell me up,
Thou haste a burning heart and aching head,
And wouldst not need much coaxing to the task
To lap the mirror of Narcissus dry."

I stood all fix'd to hear them.—"Little more
Would make me quarrel with thee; so be warn'd,"
Cried Virgil:—when I heard him speak in warmth,
I turn'd about, and color'd with such shame,
The very thought brings back the blush upon me.
Like one who dreams of harm befalling him,
And dreaming wishes it may *be* a dream,
Desiring that which *is* as though it *were not*,
So I, unable to excuse myself
(For I stood mute), excused myself the more,
Unwittingly.—"Less shame than thine might make
Atonement for a greater fault than thine,"

My Master said, " so cast away thy sadness ;
And know that I am ever at thy side ;
If fortune brings thee where such knaves fall out,
— To love their broils betrays a base-born mind."

Dell' Inferno, canto xxx.

DANTE AND BEATRICE.

There is no circumstance in the whole compass of the *Divina commedia* more exquisitely imagined than the *unfelt* swiftness with which Dante and Beatrice, by the mere act of volition on their part, are transported from planet to planet in the *Paradiso*; nor is the *evidence* of their *arrival* at each new stage, in the increased loveliness of the lady to the eyes of the poet, less delicately conceived.

I FELT not our ascension to that star,
But soon of this my lady gave me warning,
For she had grown more beautiful.
Del Paradiso, canto viii.

Their first flight from the Hill of Purgatory was to the moon. Their entrance within the sphere of "that eternal pearl" is thus described.

The native-born and everlasting thirst
For that pure realm, resembling God himself,
Carried us thither, swift as move the heavens.

My lady look'd aloof, and I on her
Then, in as brief a space as, on the string,
An arrow rests, escapes, and flits away,*

* The same comparison is used on another like occasion, with a singular though minute variation.

And as an arrow hits the mark, before
The cord hath ceased to tremble on the bow,
Thus had we reach'd the second region.
Del Paradiso, canto v.

I found myself transported, and arrived,
Where a strange thing surprised me; but my guide,
From whom nought in my heart could be conceal'd,
Turn'd, with a sweet and gracious countenance,
Exclaiming, "Now, thank God! that we have reach'd
The nearest star." * — Methought a lucid, dense,
And brilliant cloud, like diamond, which the sun
Transpierces, compass'd us on every side:
Within the orb of that eternal pearl,
We enter'd, — as a ray of light pervades
The crystal wave, united yet unbroken."

Del Paradiso, canto ii.

The sign which spiritual intelligences in heaven give of their desire to converse with the travellers that visit their respective abodes, by shining out from among their companions with intenser lustre, is of the same happy character of thought with the idea of Beatrice's beauty brightening as she mounts from sphere to sphere.

She ceased, and seem'd to enter a new round
Within the wheel where she revolved before; †
That other ardor, known to me already,
Now flash'd out marvellously upon my sight,
Like a fine ruby smitten by the sun;
For joy in heaven brings splendor, as it brings
Laughter on earth; — but, in the abyss of hell,
Horror grows blacker as the mind more sad.

Del Paradiso, canto ix.

* The moon.

† A mystic dance, most curiously described in the original, in which the celestials are engaged.

THE RIVER OF LIFE.

The greater part of the *Paradiso*, — while it exemplifies, almost beyond example, the power of human language to vary a few ideas and images in themselves so simple, pure, and hallowed, that they hardly can be altered from their established associations without being degraded, — shows also the utter impotence of any other terms than those which Scripture has employed "as in a glass darkly," — and who can *there* add light? — to body forth what eye hath not seen, ear heard, neither hath entered into the heart of man to conceive. One elaborate specimen (however defective the translation may be) will elucidate this failure even in the noble original, which, like its ineffable theme, in this part is "dark with excessive light." The poet here copies more directly than he is wont from the sacred Oracles; or, as in the sublime simile of the rock, illustrates his subject with not unworthy natural objects; at the same time, with characteristic ingenuousness, he explains his own feelings on beholding "things which it is not lawful for a man to utter."

As sudden lightning dissipates the sight,
And leaves the eye unable to discern
The plainest objects, — living light so flash'd
Around me, and involved me in a veil
Of such effulgence, that I *ceased to see.*
"Thus Love, which soothes this heaven, all kindly fits
The torch to take his flame!" * — These few, brief words
Had scarcely reach'd mine ear, when I perceived
Power from on high diffuse such virtue through me,
And so rekindle vision, that no flame,

* Beatrice addresses this remark to Dante.

However pure, could 'scape mine eyes.
I saw
Light, like a river clear as crystal, flowing
Between two banks with wondrous spring adorn'd;
While from the current issued vivid sparks,
That fell among the flowers on either hand,
Glitter'd like rubies set in gold, and then,
As if intoxicate with sweetest odors,
Replunged themselves into the mystic flood,
Whence, as one disappear'd, another rose.

"The intense desire that warms and stirs thy thoughts
To understand what thou beholdest, yields
More joy to me, the more it urges thee;
But ere such noble thirst can be assuaged,
Behoves thee first to drink of this clear fount."
The sun that lights mine eyes * thus spake, and added:
—"Yon stream, those jewels flitting to and fro,
And all the joyance of these laughing flowers,
Are shadowy emblems of realities,
Not dark themselves, but the defect is thine,
Who hast not yet obtain'd due strength of vision."

Ah! then, no infant, startled out of sleep,
Long past his time, springs to the mother's milk
More eagerly than o'er that stream I bow'd,
To make more perfect lustres of mine eyes,

* Beatrice.

Which, when the fringes of their lids had touch'd it,
Seem'd, from a line, collapsed into a round.
— As maskers, when they cast their visors off,
Appear new persons, stript of such disguise,
The sparks and flowers assumed sublimer forms,*
And both the courts of heaven were open'd round me.

O splendor of the Deity! by which
The lofty triumph of thy real reign
I saw, — give power to paint it *as* I saw.

There is a light, which renders visible
The Maker to the creature who desires
Felicity in seeing Him alone:
— Though but a ray of uncreated glory,
Sent from the fountain-head of life and power,
It forms a circle, whose circumference
Would be too wide a girdle for the sun:
And, as a cliff in water, from its foot,
Looks down upon its height in that broad mirror,
And seems therein contemplating its beauty,
What verdure clothes, what flowers its flanks adorn,
So, standing round about that sea of glass,
As many souls as earth hath sent to heaven,
Upon ten thousand thrones and more, beheld
Their happy semblances reflected there.

* They were transfigured from symbols into their spiritual identities; and, as intimated below, the sparks were the souls of all the saints who had been removed in past ages to the bliss of heaven.

If, round its lowest stem such pomp appear,
What must the full-expanded foliage show
Of that celestial rose?* and yet my sight,
Through its whole amplitude and elevation,
Gazed unbewilder'd; yea, at once took in
The measure and the amount of all that joy.

Del Paradiso, canto XXX.

* This refers to a dry conceit, which runs through much of the *Paradiso*, arranging the happy spirits throughout the various heavens, in different forms, such as an eagle, a cross, etc., and here a rose.

THE PORTAL OF HELL.

Awfully contrasted with the foregoing dazzling spectacle, but far more real in its picturesque and imaginable grandeur, is the famous description of the entrance upon the infernal regions.

"THROUGH me, ye go into the doleful city,
Through me, ye go into eternal pain,
Through me, ye go among the lost for ever:
'Twas justice moved my Founder; Power divine,
Infinite Wisdom and primeval Love,
Ordain'd and fix'd me here. Before me nought
That is existed, save eternal things,
And I unto eternity endure;
— Abandon every hope, all ye that enter!"

These words in sombre colors I beheld
Inscribed upon the summit of a portal:
"'Tis a hard sentence, Master!" I exclaim'd:
When he, like one of ready speech, replied;
"Leave all mistrust, all base misgiving here,
We now have reach'd the place of which I told thee,
Where thou shalt see the miserable throngs,
Who mourn the loss of intellectual good."

Then straightway, in his hand enclasping mine,
With brightening countenance that cheer'd my heart,
He led me down among the things of darkness: —

There sighs, and groans, and lamentable wailings,
So rang throughout that region without star,
That on the threshold I began to weep:
Horrible tongues, discordant languages,
Words full of dolor, accents of sharp anger,
Shrill and hoarse voices, sounds of smitten hands,
Rose in wild tumult, eddying through the gloom,
Like sands before the whirlwind of the desert.

Dell' Inferno, canto iii.

ANTEUS.

Dante and Virgil, in the lowest gulf but one, find the ancient giants bound on rocks or wedged in caverns. From one of these they solicit help, namely,—a lift downward into the last abyss, where Lucifer (three-faced, and eternally worrying at each of his mouths, Judas Iscariot, Brutus, and Cassius,) is embedded in adamantine ice. The negotiation is conducted with great *finesse* on the part of Virgil, who assails the monster on his weak side, the "*laudum immensa cupido*," unextinguished even there, where "hope never comes;" the poet himself, at the same time, betraying, though from the lips of his guide, that pride of conscious power to praise or give renown, which often, and unexpectedly throws a passing glory over his human nature, even when the infirmity of the latter is most frankly confessed.

— We journey'd on, and reach'd Anteus,
Who stood above the pit's mouth five good ells,
Besides his head. — "O thou! who in the field
Of fortune, that made Scipio glory's heir,
When Hannibal with all his veterans fled,
Didst catch an hundred lions for thy prey;
And 't is believed, that, in their war with heaven,
Hadst thou been with thy brethren they had triumph'd,
— *Land us below* — (nay, scowl not thus askance) —
Where cold congeals Cocytus. Force us not
Aid to implore of Tithyus or of Typhon:
This man can give thee what ye covet here;
Bow then, nor grin upon us like a griffin; *

* "Torcer lo grifo," an Italian phrase for "to make an ugly face."

He yet can make thee famous through the world,
For he still lives, and counts on length of days,
If grace remove him not before his time.

So spake my Master, and in haste the giant
Stretch'd forth the hand, whose gripe cramp'd Hercules,
To take us up: — when Virgil felt his grasp,
"Hither," he cried, "come hither, let me hold thee;"
He caught me, and we both became one burden.
Then, as the tower of Carisenda seems
Itself in motion, to the eye beneath,
When a cloud sails above its leaning top;
So seem'd Anteus, when I watch'd him bend,
And wish'd myself elsewhere; but easily,
Down in the gulf that gorges Lucifer
And Judas, he deposited us twain:
Nor stooping staid he, but anon, erect,
Rose like a ship's mast from the rocking surge.

Dell' Inferno, canto xxxi.

CAIN.

If, in the scene with Anteus, the emphasis of silence, and the perspicuity of graphic delineation, are happily exemplified, in the following brief passage the force of mere sounds (where no image or personification is presented to the eye) is made to produce a surprising effect. On one of the sloping mazes of the spiral Hill of Purgatory, the travellers having parted with some agreeable company, which had long engaged them, it is said: —

WE knew those friendly spirits heard us going,
Their silence therefore show'd our path was right:
Now left alone, proceeding on our journey,
Like lightning when it rends the region, rush'd
A voice beside us, lamentably crying,
"Ah! every one that findeth me shall slay me!" *
And then it fled, like thunder that explodes,
All in a moment, from the riven cloud:
— Scarce from that sound our ears had truce, when lo!
Brake forth another, with astounding peal,
"I am Aglauros who was turned to stone." †
Closer behind the poet's back I cower'd,
— Then was the air in every quarter still.

Dell' Purgatorio, canto xiv.

* Genesis iv. 14. † Ovid. Metam. lib. ii.

FARINATA.

In the tenth canto of the "Inferno," where heretics are described as being tormented in tombs of fire, the lids of which are suspended over them till the day of judgment, Dante finds Farinata D'Uberti, an illustrious commander of the *Ghibellines* (the adherents of the emperor,) who, at the battle of Monte Aperto, in 1260, had so utterly defeated the *Guelfs* (the Pope's party) of Florence, that the city lay at the mercy of its enemies, by whom counsel was taken to raze it to the ground; but Farinata, because his bowels yearned towards the place of his nativity, stood up alone to oppose the barbarous design; and partly by menace — having drawn his sword in the midst of the assembly — and partly by persuasion, preserved it from destruction. Notwithstanding this patriotic interference, when the Guelfs afterwards regained the ascendency, he and his kindred were most inveterately proscribed there, and doomed to perpetual exile.

The interview between Dante and this magnanimous foe, in those

"Regions of sorrow, doleful shades, where peace
And rest can never dwell; hope never comes,
That comes to all; but torture without end
Still urges, and a fiery deluge, fed
With ever-burning sulphur unconsumed." —
(*Paradise Lost*, book i.)

is painted with transcendent power of coloring, and stern undecorated energy of style. To prepare the reader for well understanding the episode, which abruptly breaks through the order of this high dramatic scene, it is necessary to state that Cavalcante Cavalcanti, whose head appears out of an adjacent sepulchre, was the father of Guido Cavalcanti, a poet, the particular friend of Dante, and chief of the Bianchi party, who was banished during his priorship.

"O Tuscan! Thou, who, through this realm of fire,
Alive dost walk, thus courteously conversing,
Pause, if it please thee here. Thy dialect
Proclaims thy lineage from that noble land,

Which I perhaps too much have wrong'd."
Such sounds
Suddenly issued forth from one of those
Sepulchral caverns. — Tremblingly I crept
A little nearer to my guide; but he
Cried, "Turn again! what would'st thou do? Behold
'T is Farinata, that hath raised himself:
There may'st thou see him, upward from the loins."
— Already had I fix'd mine eyes on his,
Who stood, with bust and visage so erect,
As though he look'd on hell itself with scorn.
My Master then, with prompt and resolute hands,
Thrust me among the charnel-vaults towards him,
Saying: — "Thy words be plain!" When I had reach'd
His tomb-stone-foot, he look'd at me awhile
As in disdain; then loftily demanded, —
"Who were thine ancestors?"
— Eager to tell,
Nought I conceal'd, but utter'd all the truth.
Arching his brow a little, he return'd,
"Bitter antagonists of mine, of me,
And of my party, were thy sires; but twice
I scatter'd them."
"If scatter'd twice," said I,
"Once and again they came from all sides back,
— A lesson, which *thy* friends have not well learn'd."

Just then, a second figure, at his side,
Emerged to view; unveil'd above the chin,

And kneeling, as methought. — It look'd around
So wistfully, as though it hoped to find
Some other with me ; but, that hope dispell'd,
Weeping it spake: — "If through this dungeon-gloom
Grandeur of genius guide thy venturous way,
My son! — Where is he? — and why not with *thee?*"

Then I to him: — "Not of myself I came;
He who awaits me yonder brought me hither,
— One whom perhaps thy Guido held in scorn." *
His speech and form of penance had already
Taught me his name; my words were therefore pointed.
Upstarting he exclaim'd, — "How? — saidst thou *held?*
Lives he not then? and doth not heaven's sweet light
Fall on his eyes?" — when I was slow to answer,
Backward he sunk and re-appear'd no more.

Meanwhile that other most majestic form,
Near which I stood, neither changed countenance,
Nor turn'd his neck, nor lean'd to either side:
"And if," quoth he, our first debate resuming,
"They have not well that lesson learn'd, the thought

* Alluding, it is supposed, to the fact that Guido had forsaken poetry for philosophy, or preferred the latter so much to the former as to think lightly of Virgil himself in comparison with Aristotle.

Torments me more than this infernal bed:
And yet, not fifty times *her* changing face,
Who here reigns sovereign, shall be re-illumined,
Ere *thou* shalt know how hard that lesson is.*
— But tell me — so may'st thou return in peace
To the dear world above! — why are thy people
In all their acts so mad against my race?"

"The slaughter and discomfiture," said I,
"That turn'd the river red at Mont' Aperto,
Have caused such dire proscriptions in our temples."

He shook his head, deep-sighing, and rejoin'd:
"I was not *there* alone, nor without cause
Engaged with others; but I *was* alone,
And stood in her defence with open brow,
When all our council, with one voice, decreed,
That Florence should be razed from her foundation.'

"So may thy kindred find repose, as thou
Shalt loose a knot which hath entangled me!"
Thus I adjured him: — "Ye foresee what time
(If rightly I have learn'd) will bring to pass,
But to the present, otherwise, are blind."

"We see, like him that hath an evil eye,
Far distant things," said he, "so highest God
Enlightens us, but yet when they approach,

* He foretells Dante's own expulsion from his country, within fifty lunar months.

Or when they are, our intellect falls short;
Nor can we know, save by report from others,
Aught of the state of man below the sun:
Hence may'st thou comprehend, how all our knowl-
edge
Shall cease for ever from that point, which shuts
The portal of the future."
At that moment,
Compunction smote me for my recent fault,
And I cried out: — "O tell that fallen one,
His son is yet among the living: — say,
That if I falter'd to reply at first,
With that assurance, 't was because my thoughts
Were harass'd by the doubt which thou hast solved."

Dell' Inferno, canto x.

The reader of these lines (however inferior the translation may be) cannot have failed to perceive by what natural action and speech, the paternal anxiety of Cavalcanti respecting his son is indicated. On his bed of torture he hears a voice which he knows to be that of his son's friend: he starts up, looks eagerly about, as expecting to see his son; but observing the friend only, he at once interrupts the dialogue between Dante and Farinata, and in broken exclamations inquires concerning him. The poet happening to employ the past tense of a verb in reference to what his "Guido" might have done, the miserable parent instantly lays hold of that minute circumstance, as an intimation of his death, and asks hurried questions of which he dreads the answers, precisely in the manner of Macduff, when he learns from the messenger that his wife and children had been murdered by Macbeth. Dante hesitating to reply, Cavalcanti takes the worst for granted, falls back in despair, and appears not again. Thus with him

"Even from the tomb the voice of nature cries."

The poet, however, at the close of the scene, unexpectedly

recurs to his own fault with the tenderness of compunction and delicacy due to an unfortunate being, whom he had unintentionally agonized by his silence, and sends a message to the old man that his son yet lives. Contrasted with this trembling sensibility of a father's affection, stronger than death, and outfeeling the pains of hell, is the proud, calm, patient dignity of Farinata, who, though wounded to the quick by the sarcastic retort of Dante, at the instant when the discourse was interrupted, stands unmoved in mind, in look, in posture, till the episode is ended; and then, without the slightest allusion to it, he takes up the suspended argument at the last words of his opponent, as though his thoughts had been all the while ruminating on the disgrace of his friends, the afflictions of his family, and the inextinguishable enmity of his countrymen against himself. His noble rejoinder, on Dante's reference to the carnage at Monte Aperto, as the cause of his people's implacability, is above all praise. Indeed it would be difficult to point out in ancient or modern tragedy, a passage of more sublimity or pathos, in which so few words express so much, yet leave more to be imagined by any one who has "a human heart," as the whole of this scene in the original Italian exhibits.

END OF VOL III.

www.ingramcontent.com/pod-product-compliance
Lightning Source LLC
LaVergne TN
LVHW020210110826

845151LV00003B/660

* 9 7 8 1 4 2 5 5 3 4 8 1 3 *